Pocket Rough Guide

LISBON

written and researched by

MATTHEW HANCOCK

Contents

<< SUNSET OVER ALFAMA
< DECORATIVE PAVEMENT, ROSSIO SQUARE

INTRODUCTION TO
LISBON

Set across a series of hills overlooking the broad estuary of the Rio Tejo (River Tagus), Lisbon's stunning location and effortless beauty immediately strike most first-time visitors. It's an instantly likeable place, a big city, with a population of around two million, but one that remains human enough in pace and scale to be easily taken in over a long weekend. That said, many visitors visit again and again, smitten by a combination of old-world charm and cosmopolitan vibrancy that makes it one of Europe's most exciting cities.

RUA AUGUSTA, BAIXA

Best place for alfresco dining

The best way to soak up Lisbon's atmosphere is to grab an outdoor table and sit back with a coffee or something more substantial. Hidden in the heart of the Alfama, *Lautasco* has tables in a tranquil courtyard (see p.48), or enjoy a pizza-with-a-view at riverside *Casanova* (see p.48). It is harder to find a lovelier lunch spot than the gardens of the Museu Nacional de Arte Antiga (see p.78). Alternatively, head to one of Lisbon's squares or *miradouros* (viewpoints) such as *Portas do Sol* (above, see p.50), many of which have cafés, bars or restaurants.

Although now one of the EU's least expensive capitals, Lisbon was once one of the continent's wealthiest, controlling a maritime empire that stretched from Brazil to Macau. The iconic Torre de Belém, Mosteiro dos Jerónimos and dramatic Moorish castle survive from these times, though many other buildings were destroyed in the Great Earthquake of 1755. Today, much of the historic centre – the Baixa, Chiado and Bairro Alto – dates from the late eighteenth and nineteenth centuries. The biggest attraction in these quarters is the street life: nothing beats watching the city's comings and goings from a pavement café over a powerful bica coffee or Portuguese beer.

If you're fit enough to negotiate its hills, Lisbon is a great place to explore on foot: get off the beaten track and you'll find atmospheric neighbourhoods sheltering aromatic *pastelarias* (patisseries), traditional shops, and shuttered houses faced with beautiful azulejo tiles. Getting around by public transport can be fun in itself, whether you're cranking uphill on one of the city's ancient trams, riding a ferry across the Rio Tejo, or speeding across town on the metro, whose stations are decorated with adventurous contemporary art.

Lisbon also boasts excellent museums – from the Gulbenkian, with its amazing collection of arts through the ages, to the Berardo, whose modern paintings are the envy of Europe, via the Museu Nacional de Arte Antiga, the national gallery, with top

When to visit

Lisbon is comfortably warm from April to October (average daily temperature 20–28ºC), with cooling Atlantic breezes making it less hot than Mediterranean cities on the same latitude. Most Lisbon residents take their holidays in July and August (27–28ºC), which means that some shops, bars and restaurants close for the period and the local beaches are heaving. Lower temperatures of 22–26ºC mean September and October are good times to visit, as is June, when the city enjoys its main festivals. Even in midwinter it is rarely cold and, as one of Europe's sunniest capitals, the sun usually appears at some stage to light up the city.

Portuguese and European masterpieces.

Lisbon's eclectic nightlife scene ranges from the traditional fado clubs of the Alfama district to glitzy venues in the Bairro Alto or Santos, many of them playing African and Brazilian beats influenced by immigrants from Portugal's former colonies.

Elsewhere, the city offers a fascinating mishmash of the traditional and cutting edge: chequered tiled bars full of old-timers supping brandies adjacent to boutiquey clubs pumping out the latest sounds; tiny *tascas* with bargain menus scrawled on boards rubbing shoulders with designer restaurants eyeing the latest Michelin awards, and tiny stores that wrap handmade products in paper and string overlooking gleaming shopping malls.

Should city life begin to pall, take the train out to the beautiful hill-top town of Sintra whose lush wooded heights and royal palaces comprise a UNESCO World Heritage Site. Alternatively, the lively resorts of Estoril and Cascais are just half an hour away, with the best beaches lying south of the city, along the Costa da Caparica, where Atlantic breakers crash on kilometre after kilometre of superb dune-backed sands.

SANTA ENGRÁCIA

LISBON AT A GLANCE

>> EATING

You are never far from a restaurant in Lisbon. For diversity, head to the **Bairro Alto** district where you'll find an eclectic array of inexpensive diners alongside ultra-hip venues. The **Baixa** caters to Lisbon's workers and has a whole street, Rua das Portas de Santo Antão, largely given over to seafood restaurants. International flavours can be sampled by the Tejo at the **Parque das Nações** and the dockside developments at **Santa Apolónia** and **Doca de Santo Amaro**, while fashionistas head to the cool haunts of **Santos**. Some of the best dining experiences, however, are in local neighbourhood restaurants highlighted in the guide.

>> DRINKING

The most historic cafés are scattered throughout the **Baixa** and **Chiado** districts where you'll find locals getting their caffeine fixes throughout the day. You can also get beer, wine or food at these places, though many bars only open after dark (see below). Portuguese beers – largely Sagres and Superbock – are inexpensive and recommended, while local wines are invariably excellent. Worth sampling too are local brandies; the white variety of port, which makes an excellent aperitif; and a powerful cherry brandy called *ginginha* – several bars in the Baixa specialize in the stuff. Finally, don't miss trying a *caipirinha*, a Brazilian cocktail made from distilled sugar cane, sugar and lime juice.

>> SHOPPING

Suburban Lisbon has some of Europe's largest shopping malls, but the city centre is a pleasing mixture of quirky local stores and smaller independent outlets. The top end of **Avenida da Liberdade** features the likes of Armani and Luis Vuitton, while **Chiado** is the place to head for glass and jewellery. Antique shops cluster round **São Bento**, **Príncipe Real** and **Campo de Santa Clara**, while off-the-wall clothing and accessories are to be found in the independent boutiques of the **Bairro Alto**. **Santos** has become the district of design, with several stores dedicated to contemporary jewellery and cutting-edge home products.

>> NIGHTLIFE

Lisbon has a pulsating nightlife, with the highest concentration of clubs and bars in the **Bairro Alto**. Many locals prefer the less frenetic vibe of the **Santos** district which has a handful of cool clubs and happening bars, while the city's biggest clubs are to be found near the river, especially Lux near **Santa Apolónia** and the upmarket venues of **Alcântara**. There are various excellent live music venues, with the **Bairro Alto** and **Alfama** famed for their fado houses.

OUR RECOMMENDATIONS FOR WHERE TO EAT, DRINK AND SHOP ARE LISTED AT THE END OF EACH PLACES CHAPTER.

Day One in Lisbon

☕ **Café Suiça** > p.37. Join the bustle of the central square's best café, the best place to people-watch.

2 The Baixa > p.30. Head down main Rua da Augusta and explore the characterful streets and cafés of the Baixa grid.

3 Chiado > p.52. Stroll up Rua do Carmo and Rua Garrett where many of Lisbon's best shops can be found.

🍽 **Lunch** > p.57. At *Casa Liège*, where local workers fill up on hearty cuisine.

4 Tram #28 > p.45. This is Lisbon's most famous tram route, grinding back through the Baixa and up towards the Castelo through the Alfama.

5 Castelo de São Jorge > p.42. Walk up to the ruined Moorish castle, the heart of historic Lisbon.

6 Alfama > p.45. Take the steps into the Alfama, Lisbon's village within a city where traditional life still holds sway.

7 Casa do Fado > p.46. Gain an insight into the history and sounds of Portugal's distinctive music at this informative museum.

🍽 **Dinner** > p.51. Try one of the Alfama's fado houses, where you can dine while listening to live music; *A Baiuca* is a good place to start.

🍷 **Drinks** > p.50. End the night by the riverside at *Lux*, one of Europe's coolest clubs.

Day Two in Lisbon

1 Museu Calouste Gulbenkian
> p.99. Take the metro to this superb museum displaying arts and crafts from the time of the Ancient Egyptians to the French Impressionists.

2 Parque Eduardo VII > p.100. It is a short walk from the museums to Lisbon's main central park famed for its Estufas – hothouses filled with exotic plants.

3 Cais do Sodré > p.54. Take the metro or a bus to Cais do Sodré where you'll find the Mercado da Ribeira, Lisbon's main market.

Lunch > p.59. Have lunch and people watch at the arty *Café Tati*, behind the market.

4 Mosteiro dos Jerónimos > p.87. Take the tram to Belém's fantastic monastery, built to give thanks to the success of Portugal's great navigators.

5 Berardo Collection > p.89. Don't miss this superb collection of modern art, featuring the likes of Andy Warhol and Paula Rego.

6 Torre de Belém > p.90. Climb the elaborate sixteenth-century riverside tower that has become the symbol of the city.

Dinner > p.67. *Cervejaria Trindade*, a cavernous beer hall serving great seafood.

Drinks > p.70. Stick around the Bairro Alto and wait for the nightlife to crank up at its hundreds of little bars and clubs.

Lisbon **viewpoints**

Built on seven hills, Lisbon has some fantastic miradouros, or viewpoints, each with its own distinctive outlook over the city's skyline – here we list the best, along with some other dramatic vantage points.

1 Miradouro da Santa Luzia > p.42. The best place to see over the terracotta rooftops of the Alfama and the eastern riverfront.

2 São Vicente de Fora > p.44. Climb to the top of this historic church for dizzy views over the eastern city from its extensive roof.

3 Castelo > p.42. Not quite Lisbon's highest hill, but climb around the ramparts to see all sides of the city.

4 Parque Eduardo VII > p.100. The top of the park offers an exhilarating panorama encompassing Lisbon and beyond.

Lunch > p.104. Chill out by a lake at *A Linha d'Água*, which serves good-value buffet lunches at the top of the park.

5 Miradouro da Graça > p.44. Superb views over the Castelo and the city beyond can be had from this breezy terrace by the church of Graça.

6 Miradouro de São Pedro de Alcântara > p.60. A broad, tree-lined

viewpoint from where you can gaze down on the Baixa and the castle opposite.

7 Miradouro de Santa Catarina. > p.54. Tucked-away *miradouro* with sweeping views over the Tejo, a popular hangout for Lisbon's alternative crowd.

Dinner > p.58. *Noobai* is hidden under the lip of Miradouro de Santa Catarina and serves inexpensive food and drinks.

Lisbon **for families**

Lisbon is very family-friendly and children are welcomed everywhere. Below are some of the best attractions for those with kids of any age.

1 Tram rides > p.45. Take the famous tram #28 for the classic run, though the other routes can be just as fun with fewer crowds.

2 Oceanário > p.108. One of the largest in Europe, this stunning building has sharks, rays, otters, penguins and fish galore.

3 Pavilhão do Conhecimento > p.108. This science museum has fantastic hands-on experiments and challenges for people of all ages, together with informative exhibits.

🍴 Lunch > p.111. The traffic-free restaurants of Parque das Nações are great for kids – one of the best places for an inexpensive lunch is *Azul Profundo*.

4 Boat trips > p.142. Take a leisurely cruise up the Tejo to see the city from the river.

5 Museu da Marioneta > p.77. From medieval marionettes to contemporary satirical puppets, this museum trumpets an art form that satisfied children long before computer games.

6 Caparica > p.125. Lisbon's best beaches are just south of the city, great at any time of the year for a walk or day by the sea.

7 Sintra > p.112. Horse and carriage rides, castles and fantasy palaces make this a great day out for any family.

8 Jardim Zoológico > p.101. Along with the usual array of caged beasties, you'll find rides, games and even a cable car to peer down from.

🍴 Dinner > p.35. With lots of space, early-opening *Bom Jardim* has tables inside and out, affordable food that kids love, and waiters who are usually extremely child-friendly.

The big sights

1 Torre de Belém This fabulously ornate tower was built to defend the mouth of the Tejo River and is now the tourist board's icon for Lisbon. **> p.90**

2 Mosteiro dos Jerónimos Packed with flamboyant Manueline architectural features, this sixteenth-century monastery commemorates Vasco da Gama's discovery of a sea route to India. **> p.87**

3 Castelo de São Jorge Once a Moorish castle and later a palace and prison, the *castelo* is now one of Lisbon's best viewpoints. **> p.42**

4 Alfama A maze of steps and tortuous alleys where life continues much as it has for centuries. **> p.45**

5 Oceanário A spectacular oceanarium, with a massive high-tech central tank containing everything from sea otters to sharks. **> p.108**

Museums and galleries

1 Museu Calouste Gulbenkian Virtually an A–Z of the history of art, from the Mesopotamians to the Impressionists, all set in a delightful park. **> p.99**

2 Berardo Collection See work by some of the biggest names in modern art from Bacon to Rothko, amassed by wealthy Madeiran Joe Berardo. > **p.89**

3 Museu da Marinha A giant overview of the Portuguese maritime explorations, battles and boats from replicas to full-size galleons. > **p.88**

4 Museu Nacional de Arte Antiga Portugal's national gallery includes works by the likes of Nuno Gonçalves and Hieronymus Bosch. > **p.76**

5 Casa das Histórias Cascais' museum building is every bit as stunning as its works of art by vibrant Portuguese contemporary artist Paula Rego. > **p.124**

Eating out

1 **Cervejaria da Trindade** The nineteenth-century beer hall is touristy but appealing, with decorative tiles, a little garden and tasty seafood. **> p.67**

2 Ribadouro
Bustling restaurant specializing in superb grilled prawns, though other dishes are equally tasty. > **p.104**

3 Tavares Lisbon's oldest and grandest restaurant also boasts a Michelin Star. > **p.58**

4 Bom Jardim, Rei dos Frangos
Not exactly glamorous but the best place in town for delicious barbecue-grilled chicken. > **p.35**

5 Rêsto do Chapitô Buzzing tapas bar/restaurant with one of the best views in the city from its outdoor terrace.> **p.50**

Nightlife

1 Lux Part-owned by John Malkovich and attracting international DJs, this is Lisbon's top club – it also boasts a beautiful rooftop terrace. **> p.50**

2 Casas de Fado There are countless fado houses, mostly in the Bairro Alto or Alfama; *Tasca do Chico* is a great place to start. > **p.73**

3 Enoteca This hidden wine bar has cool stone rooms in a cavernous former bathhouse. > **p.70**

4 A Ginginha Tiny bar serving *ginginha* (cherry brandy) since 1840: order it with or without the stone to kick start an evening out. > **p.37**

5 Portas Largas Ancient *tasca* (tavern) with original marble counter and tables, but a distinctly modern clientele often spilling out onto the street. > **p.72**

Cafés

1 Antiga Confeitaria de Belém This cavernous place serves the best *pastéis de nata* in town – get there early to beat the queues. **> p.93**

2 Suiça
Perennially popular café with outdoor tables facing Lisbon's two main squares.
> p.37

3 Café Versailles Wonderful café with waiters in bow ties and a fleet of coiffured women devouring cakes and sandwiches. **> p.105**

4 A Brasileira The city's most famous café, opened in 1905 and the hub of café society ever since. **> p.58**

5 Pois Café Homely, high-ceilinged café in the heart of Alfama, serving fresh food, cakes and healthy snacks and with comfy sofas to lounge on.
> p.49

Shopping

1 Mercado da Ribeira Pungent and colourful food market, with regional crafts, food and a restaurant upstairs. **> p.54**

2 Armazéns do Chiado Central Lisbon's most appealing shopping centre, with top-floor cafés offering fine city views. **> p.56**

3 Manuel Tavares This traditional Baixa shop is a great place to buy port, wine, local cheese and confectionery. **> p.34**

4 Espaço Fátima Lopes Check out the latest designer clothing at this store belonging to Lisbon's queen of fashion. **> p.66**

5 Solar Albuquerque You could spend hours browsing the ceramics, tiles and antiques at this shop specializing in reclaimed items from old houses. **> p.66**

The Baixa and Rossio

The tall, imposing buildings that make up the Baixa (Lower Town, pronounced bye-sha) house some of Lisbon's most interesting shops and cafés. Many of the streets are pedestrianized and, by day, they thrum with business folk and street entertainers. When the offices close, however, the whole area is strangely quiet. Facing the river, these streets felt the full force of the 1755 earthquake that destroyed much of what was then one of Europe's wealthiest capitals. The king's minister, the Marquês de Pombal, swiftly redesigned the sector with the grid pattern that is evident today, framed by a triangle of broad squares. Praça do Comércio sits to the south, with Praça da Figueira and Rossio to the north, the latter having been the city's main square since medieval times.

PRAÇA DO COMÉRCIO

MAP P.29, POCKET MAP E13

The beautiful, arcaded Praça do Comércio represents the climax of Pombal's design. Its classical buildings were once a royal palace and the square is centred on an exuberant bronze equestrian statue of Dom José,

monarch during the earthquake and the period of the capital's rebuilding. Two of Portugal's last royals came to a sticky end in this square: in 1908 King Carlos I and his eldest son were shot dead here, clearing the way for the declaration of the Republic two years later.

Praça do Comércio's **riverfront** provides a natural focus for the area. In the hour or two before sunset people often linger in the golden light to watch the orange ferries ply between the Estação Fluvial and Barreiro on the opposite side of the Tejo. The secluded Patio da Galé, tucked into the western arcades, hosts frequent events, while the eastern arcades house the Lisbon Story Centre, an exhibition space dedicated to Lisbon's history. The square is also a major transport interchange – the starting point for tram and bus tours of the city (see p.142), as well as home to the Lisbon Welcome Centre, the city's main tourist office (see p.145).

ARCADE ON PRAÇA DO COMÉRCIO

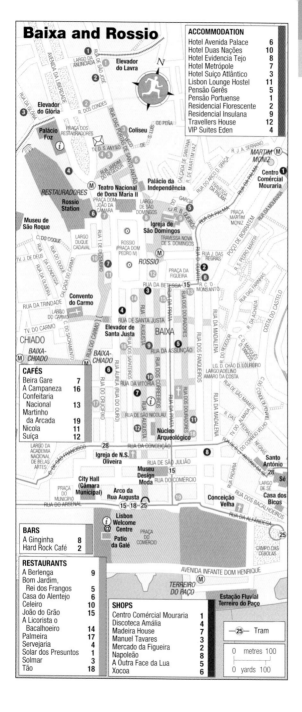

PRAÇA DO MUNICÍPIO

MAP P.29, POCKET MAP D13

The attractive, mosaic-paved Praça do Município houses the Neoclassical nineteenth-century Câmara Municipal (City Hall), where the Portuguese Republic was declared in 1910, flatteringly described by Portugal's greatest twentieth-century poet Pessoa as "one of the finest buildings in the city". The square adjoins Rua do Arsenal, an atmospheric street packed with pungent shops selling dried cod and grocers selling cheap wines, port and brandies.

ARCO DA RUA AUGUSTA AND RUA AUGUSTA

MAP P.29, POCKET MAP D11

Praça do Comércio's most prominent building is a huge arch, the Arco da Rua Augusta, adorned with statues of historical figures, including the Marquês de Pombal and Vasco da Gama. Acting as a gateway to the city, the arch was built to celebrate Lisbon's reconstruction after the earthquake, although it wasn't completed until 1873. From here, the mosaic-paved Rua Augusta is the Baixa's main pedestrianized thoroughfare, filled with shops, cafés, market stalls and buskers.

MUSEU DESIGN MODA

Rua Augusta 24 ☎ 218 886 117, ⓦ www .mude.pt. Tues–Thurs & Sun 10am–8pm, Fri–Sat 10am–10pm. Free. MAP P.29, POCKET MAP E13

Housed in a grand former bank, the Museu Design Moda is an impressive collection of design and fashion classics from the 1930s to today amassed by former stockbroker and media mogul Francisco Capelo. The museum's ever-changing exhibitions include design classics, such as

ALEXANDER McQUEEN SKIRT, MUSEU DESIGN MODA

furniture by Charles and Ray Eames and Phillipe Starck, and also features Capelo's fashion collection – haute couture from the 1950s, 1960s street fashion and the brand labelling of the 1990s. Look out for Ron Arad's "Big Easy" steel chair (1951), Frank Gehry's wiggle chair (1972) and the 1959 Vespa, while fashionistas will adore Paco Rabanne's metalized leather boots, Pierre Cardin's 1950s coats and Alexander McQueen's superb fur skirt. There's also a bookshop and café.

THE BAIXA GRID

MAP P.29, POCKET MAP D11

Pombal designed the Baixa to have three main streets dissected by nine smaller streets. Many of these streets took their names from the crafts and businesses carried out there, like Rua da Prata (Silversmiths' Street) and Rua dos Sapateiros (Cobblers' Street). Modern banks and offices have disturbed these divisions somewhat, though plenty of traditional stores remain; the central section of Rua da Conceição, for example, is still lined with shops selling

The Lisbon Earthquake

Early eighteenth-century Lisbon had been one of the most active and important ports in Europe, making the Great Earthquake of 1755 all the more tragic. The quake, which was felt as far away as Jamaica, struck Lisbon at 9.30am on November 1 (All Saints' Day), when most of the city's population was at Mass. Within the space of ten minutes there had been three major tremors and the candles of a hundred church altars had started fires that raged throughout the capital. A vast tidal wave later swept the waterfront and, in all, 40,000 of the 270,000 population died. The destruction of the city shocked the continent and prompted religious debate between philosophers Voltaire and Rousseau. For Portugal, it was a disaster that ended its capital's golden age.

beads and sequins. Some of the most interesting streets to explore are the smaller ones running south to north – Rua dos Correeiros, Rua dos Douradores and Rua dos Sapateiros. Pombal also wanted the grid's churches to blend in with his harmonious design, so much so that they are almost invisible – walk along Rua de São Julião and the facade of the church of Oliveira is barely distinguishable from the offices alongside it, though its tiled interior is delightful.

NÚCLEO ARQUEOLÓGICO

Rua dos Correeiros 9 ☎ 211 131 004. Advance bookings required. Thurs 5pm, Sat 10am–noon & 3–5pm. Free. MAP P.29, POCKET MAP E12

One of Lisbon's smallest but most fascinating museums lies beneath the Baixa's streets. The remains of Roman fish-preserving tanks, a fifth-century Christian burial place and Moorish ceramics can all be seen in the tiny Núcleo Arqueológico, containing the remains of excavations revealed during building work on the BCP bank. Most exhibits are viewed through glass floors or from cramped walkways under the modern bank during a 30- to 45-minute tour. Pombal actually rebuilt most of the Baixa on a riverbed, and you can even see the wooden piles driven into the waterlogged soil to support the buildings, the same device that is used in Venice.

writers, though many of the artists' haunts were converted to banks in the 1970s. Nevertheless, the outdoor seats of the square's remaining cafés are perennially popular meeting points. On the northwestern side of the square, there's a horseshoe-shaped entrance to Rossio station, a mock-Manueline complex with the train platforms an escalator ride above the street-level entrances.

TEATRO NACIONAL DE DONA MARIA II

Rossio ☎ 213 250 800, ⓦ www.teatro-dmaria .pt. MAP P.29, POCKET MAP D10

Rossio's biggest concession to grandeur is the Teatro Nacional de Dona Maria II built along its north side in the 1840s, and heavily restored after a fire in 1964. Inside there is a good café. Prior to the earthquake, the Inquisitional Palace stood on this site, in front of which public hangings and autos-da-fé (ritual burnings of heretics) took place.

IGREJA DE SÃO DOMINGOS

Largo de São Domingos. MAP P.29, POCKET MAP D11

The Igreja de São Domingos stands on the site of the thirteenth-century Convento de São Domingos, where sentences were read out during the Inquisition. The convent was destroyed in the earthquake of 1755, though its portal was reconstructed soon after as part of the current Dominican church. For over a century it was the venue for royal marriages and christenings, though it lost this role after the declaration of the Republic and was then gutted by a fire in the 1950s. Some say the fire purged some unsavoury acts that took place on the spot in the past, such as the massacre

ELEVADOR DE SANTA JUSTA

Rua de Santa Justa. Daily: Oct–May 7am–10pm, June–Sept 7am–11pm. €5 return. MAP P.29, POCKET MAP D11

Raul Mésnier's extraordinary and eccentric Elevador de Santa Justa was built in 1902 by a disciple of Eiffel. Its giant lift whisks you 32m up the inside of a latticework metal tower, to deposit you on a platform high above the Baixa. Before taking the upper exit on to the Largo do Carmo (see p.61), head up the dizzy spiral staircase to the pricey rooftop café with great views over the city.

ROSSIO

MAP P.29, POCKET MAP C11

Praça Dom Pedro IV (popularly known as Rossio) has been the city's main square since medieval times and it remains the hub of commercial Lisbon. Its central space sparkles with Baroque fountains and polished, mosaic-cobbled pavements. During the nineteenth century, Rossio's plethora of cafés attracted Lisbon's painters and of New Christians which began here in 1506. It was reopened in 1997 after partial restoration to replace the seats and some statues; however, the rest of the cavernous interior and the scarred pillars remain powerfully atmospheric.

PRAÇA DA FIGUEIRA

MAP P.29, POCKET MAP D11

Praça da Figueira is an historic square (once the site of Lisbon's main market), though the recent addition of an underground car park has detracted from its former grandeur. Nevertheless, it is slightly quieter than Rossio, and its cafés offer appealing views of the green slopes of the Castelo de São Jorge.

PRAÇA DOS RESTAURADORES

MAP P.29, POCKET MAP C10

The elongated Praça dos Restauradores (Square of the Restorers) takes its name from the renewal of independence from Spain in 1640. To the north of the square, the **Elevador da Glória** offers access to the Bairro Alto (see p.60); south sits the superb Art Deco frontage of the old Eden cinema, now an apartment-hotel (see p.131). The square is dominated by the pink Palácio de Foz on the western side, which housed the Ministry of Propaganda under the Salazar regime (1932–74) but is now home to the Portuguese Tourist Office (see p.145) and tourist police station. During the week it is sometimes possible to visit the palace's ornate upper floors (enquire at the tourist office).

RUA DAS PORTAS DE SANTO ANTÃO

MAP P.29, POCKET MAP D10

The pedestrianized Rua das Portas de Santo Antão is well

known for its seafood restaurants. Despite the tourist trappings – this and the adjacent Rua Jardim Regedor are the only places in town you're likely to get waiters trying to smooth-talk you into their premises – it is worth eating here at least once to sample its seafood. The street is also home to several theatres, and the domed **Coliseu dos Recreios** at #96 (☎ 213 240 580, ⓦ www.coliseulisboa.com), which opened in 1890 as a circus but is now one of Lisbon's main concert venues.

ELEVADOR DO LAVRA

Largo da Anunciada. Mon–Sat 7am–9pm, Sun 9am–9pm. €3.50 return. MAP P.29, POCKET MAP K5

Rua das Portas de Santo Antão ends next to where another of the city's classic *elevadores*, Elevador do Lavra, begins its ascent. The funicular opened in 1882 and is Lisbon's least tourist-frequented *elevador*. At the top a short walk down Travessa do Torel takes you to **Jardim do Torel**, a tiny park offering exhilarating views over the city.

ELEVADOR DO LAVRA

Shops

CENTRO COMÉRCIAL MOURARIA

Largo Martim Moniz. Most shops Mon–Sat
10am–7pm. MAP P.29, POCKET MAP E10
The rather drab concrete
expanse of Largo Martim
Moniz – named after a Christian knight who died battling
the Moors – is enlivened by
the city's tackiest and most
run-down shopping centre,
sufficiently atmospheric to
warrant a look around its six
levels (three of them underground). Hundreds of small,
family-run stores selling
Indian fabrics and oriental and
African produce, alongside an
aromatic collection of cafés on
Level –3, give an insight into
Lisbon's ethnic communities,
perfect if you need an Afro
haircut or a sari.

DISCOTECA AMÁLIA

Rua Áurea 272. Mon–Sat 9.30am–1pm &
2.30–7pm. MAP P.29, POCKET MAP D12
A small but well-stocked shop
named after famous fado singer
Amália Rodrigues, with a good
collection of traditional Portuguese fado music. If you're
looking for a recommendation,
the English-speaking staff are
usually happy to help.

MADEIRA HOUSE

Rua Augusta 133. Mon–Fri 9am–1pm &
3–7pm, Sat 9am–1pm. MAP P.29, POCKET MAP D12
As you'd expect, linens and
embroidery from Madeira
feature, along with some
attractive ceramics, tiles and
souvenirs from the mainland.

MANUEL TAVARES

Rua da Betesga 1a. Mon–Sat
9.30am–7.30pm. MAP P.29, POCKET MAP D11
Small, century-old treasure-
trove, with a great selection of
nuts, chocolate and national
cheeses, and a basement stuffed
with vintage wines and ports,
some dating from the early
1900s.

MERCADO DA FIGUEIRA

Praça da Figueira 10b. Mon–Fri 8.30am–8pm,
Sat 8.30am–7pm. MAP P.29, POCKET MAP E11
The decorative, narrow
entrance hall gives onto a
well-stocked supermarket with
a good array of inexpensive
wines, ports and fresh produce.

NAPOLEÃO

Rua dos Fanqueiros 70. Mon–Sat
9.30am–8pm. MAP P.29, POCKET MAP E12
This spruce shop offers a great
range of quality port and
wine from all Portugal's main
regions, and its enthusiastic,
English-speaking staff can
advise on what to buy.

A OUTRA FACE DA LUA

Rua da Assunção 22. Mon–Sat 10am–8pm.
MAP P.29, POCKET MAP D12
This buzzy space specializes
in retro fashion – fab clothes,
tin toys and the like; it also has
a great attached café serving
crostini and snacks.

MERCADO PRAÇA DA FIGUEIRA

XOCOA

Rua do Crucifixo 112–114 ☎ 213 466 370.
Mon–Sat 10am–8pm. MAP P.29, POCKET MAP D12.

Chocolate shops are a relative
rarity in Portugal so this
one has become all the rage
for chocoholics. There's hot
chocolate to take away and a
staggering variety of chocolate
bars, biscuits and cakes.

Restaurants

A BERLENGA

Rua Barros Queirós 29. ☎ 213 422 703. Daily
noon–midnight. MAP P.29, POCKET MAP D10.

Atmospheric *cervejaria* with a
window displaying crabs and
seafood. Take a seat for a plate
of prawns at the bar on one
side, or sit down at the main
restaurant for good-value fish,
meat and seafood. Mains range
from €8 to €12.

BOM JARDIM, REI DOS FRANGOS

Trav. de Santo Antão 11–18 ☎ 213 424 389.
Daily noon–11.30pm. MAP P.29, POCKET MAP C10.

A bit of a Lisbon institution thanks to its spit-roast
chickens and now so popular
that it has spread into three
buildings on either side of a
pedestrianized alley. There
are plenty of tables outdoors,
too. A half chicken is yours
for around €6, though it also
serves other meat and fish at
less generous prices.

CASA DO ALENTEJO

Rua das Portas de Santo Antão 58 ☎ 213
469 231. Daily noon–3pm & 7–10.30pm. MAP
P.29, POCKET MAP D10.

A centre dedicated to Alentejan
culture with its own restaurant, "Alentejo House" has
an extravagantly decorated
interior complete with a
stunning inner courtyard and
seventeenth-century furniture.
Alentejo specialities include

CASA DO ALENTEJO

sopa à alentejana (garlic soup
with egg) and *carne de porco à
alentejana* (grilled pork with
clams) with mains from €11;
or just pop in for a drink in
the superb bar area hung with
chandeliers.

CELEIRO

Rua 1° de Dezembro 45 ☎ 210 306 000.
Mon–Sat noon–5pm, café 9am–6pm. MAP P.29,
POCKET MAP D11.

Just off Rossio, this inexpensive
self-service restaurant sits in
the basement of a health-food
supermarket and offers tasty
vegetarian spring rolls, quiches,
pizza and the like from around
€6. There's also a streetside café
offering snacks and drinks.

JOÃO DO GRÃO

Rua dos Correeiros 222–228 ☎ 213 424
757. Daily noon–3.30pm & 6–11pm. MAP P.29,
POCKET MAP D11.

One of the best in a row of
restaurants on this pedestrianized street, where appealing
outdoor tables tempt you to
sample the reasonably priced
salads, fish and rice dishes
(from €9). The marble- and
azulejo-clad interior is just as
attractive.

A LICORISTA O BACALHOEIRO

Rua dos Sapateiros 222–224 ☎ 213 431 415.
Mon–Fri 8am–8pm, Sat 8am–1pm. MAP P.29,
POCKET MAP D11

This pleasant tile-and-brick restaurant is a popular lunchtime stop, when locals flock in for inexpensive set meals or mains from around €8.

PALMEIRA

Rua do Crucifixo 69–73 ☎ 213 428 372. Mon–Fri 9am–8pm. MAP P.29, POCKET MAP O12.

This long, traditional bar-restaurant is very popular at lunchtimes, with back and side dining areas where you can enjoy terrific *petiscos* (snacks) such as smoked hams, cheeses and *leitão* (suckling pig), as well as good value full meals, with mains from €7.

SERVEJARIA

Praça dos Restauradores 62–68 ☎ 213 478 274. Daily noon–1am. MAP P.29, POCKET MAP C10.

The name is the place, like the place, a modern take on a traditional *cervejaria* (beer hall), which it pulls off well. There are beer bottles lining one wall and split-level seating where you can tuck into steaks, roasts, *bacalhau* dishes and seafood – as well as beer on tap. The modern element entails big-screen sports and slightly higher than average prices (mains €9–15).

SOLAR DOS PRESUNTOS

Rua das Portas de Santo Antão 150 ☎ 213 424 253. Mon–Sat 12.30–3.30pm & 7–11pm. MAP P.29, POCKET MAP J5

The "Manor House of Hams" is, not surprisingly, best known for its smoked ham from the Minho region in northern Portugal, served cold as a starter. There are also excellent, if expensive, rice and game dishes, not to mention a good wine list; the service can be overly formal. The daily specials are good value, otherwise mains start at around €16. Reservations are advised.

SOLMAR

Rua das Portas de Santo Antão 108 ☎ 213 423 371. Daily noon–3pm & 7–2am. MAP P.29, POCKET MAP D10

A cavernous seafood restaurant, complete with fountain and marine mosaics, worth a visit as much for the experience as for the food, which can be hit or miss. Splash out on one of the lobsters in the bubbling tanks and you shouldn't leave disappointed. Despite the high prices (most mains over €10), it's not above showing live football on giant TV screens.

TÃO

Rua dos Douradores 10 ☎ 218 850 046. Mon–Fri noon–3.30pm & 6.30–11pm. MAP P.29, POCKET MAP E12

Fashionable, very good value eastern-inspired organic restaurant, with set meals from around €5–7. Tasty vegetarian sushi, risottos, grilled aubergines and salads.

Cafés

BEIRA GARE

Rua 1° de Dezembro 5. Mon–Sat 6am–1am. MAP P.29, POCKET MAP D11

Well-established café opposite Rossio station, serving stand-up Portuguese snacks and bargain meals. Constantly busy, which is recommendation enough.

A CAMPANEZA

Rua dos Sapateiros 157. Mon–Sat 8am–7pm. MAP P.29, POCKET MAP D12

Formerly a *leitaria* (dairy shop) and still displaying the Art Nouveau decor from its past existence, this is now a simple

MARTINHO DA ARCADA

pastelaria (pastry shop), with decent inexpensive snacks and coffee.

CONFEITARIA NACIONAL

Praça da Figueira 18. Daily 9am–8pm, Oct-April closed Sun. MAP P.29, POCKET MAP D11

Opened in 1829 and little changed since, with a stand-up counter selling pastries and sweets below a mirrored ceiling. There's a little side room and outdoor seating for sit-down coffees and snacks.

MARTINHO DA ARCADA

Praça do Comércio 3. Mon–Sat 7am–11pm. MAP P.29, POCKET MAP E13

One of Lisbon's oldest café-restaurants, first opened in 1782 and declared a national monument as long ago as 1910. Over the years it has been a gambling den, a meeting place for political dissidents and, later, a more reputable hangout for politicians, writers and artists. It is now divided into a simple stand-up café and a slightly pricey restaurant. The outdoor tables under the arches are a perfect spot for a coffee and a *pastel de nata*.

NICOLA

Rossio 24. Mon–Sat 9am–10pm, Sun 10am–7pm. MAP P.29, POCKET MAP D11

The only surviving Rossio coffee house from the seventeenth century, once the haunt of some of Lisbon's great literary figures. The outdoor tables overlooking the bustle of Rossio are the best feature, though it has sacrificed much of its period interior in the name of modernization. Also has occasional live fado.

SUÍÇA

Rossio 96. Daily 7am–9pm. MAP P.29, POCKET MAP D11

Famous for its cakes and pastries; you'll have a hard job getting an outdoor table here, though there's plenty of room inside. There's more alfresco seating in Praça da Figueira.

Bars

A GINGINHA

Largo de São Domingos 8. Daily 9am–10.30pm. MAP P.29, POCKET MAP D11

Everyone should try *ginginha* – Portuguese cherry brandy – once. There's just about room in this microscopic joint to walk in, down a glassful and stagger outside to see the city in a new light.

HARD ROCK CAFÉ

Avenida da Liberdade 2. Sun–Thurs 10am–2am, Fri & Sat 10am–4am. MAP P.29, POCKET MAP C10

Peppered with rock memorabilia and complete with an upside-down car on the roof, the interior is quite a sight. It extends to the full height of the old Condes cinema from which it was hollowed out. Enjoy a drink here, though the food, pricey burgers and steaks, is standard chain fare.

The Sé, Castelo and Alfama

East of the Baixa, the streets climb past the city's ancient cathedral, or Sé, to the dramatic remains of the Castelo de São Jorge, an oasis of tranquillity high above the city. East of the castle lie two of Lisbon's most prominent churches, São Vicente de Fora and Santa Engrácia. The districts around the castle – Mouraria, Santa Cruz and particularly the Alfama – represent the oldest and most atmospheric parts of Lisbon. Down on the riverfront, Santa Apolónia, the main international train station, is situated in a revitalized area that boasts the glitzy Lux club and cruise ship terminal, a short bus ride from a fascinating tile museum.

THE SÉ

Largo da Sé ☎ 218 876 628. Daily 10am–7pm. Free. Tram#28. MAP P.40-41, POCKET MAP F.12

Lisbon's main cathedral, the Sé, was founded in 1150 to commemorate the city's Reconquest from the Moors on the site of their main mosque. It's a Romanesque structure with a

THE SÉ CATHEDRAL

suitably fortress-like appearance. The great rose window and twin towers form a simple and effective facade, although there's nothing particularly exciting inside: the building was once splendidly embellished on the orders of Dom João V, but his Rococo whims were swept away by the 1755 earthquake and subsequent restorers. All that remains is a group of Gothic tombs behind the high altar and the decaying thirteenth-century **cloister** (Mon–Sat 10am–7pm, Sun 2–7pm; €2.50). This has been heavily excavated, revealing the remains of a sixth-century Roman house and Moorish public buildings.

The Baroque **Treasury** (Mon–Sat 10am–5pm; €2.50) holds a small museum of treasures including the relics of Saint Vincent, brought to Lisbon in 1173 in a boat that was piloted by ravens, according to legend. Ravens were kept in the cloisters for centuries afterwards, but the tradition halted when the last one died in 1978. To this day, the birds remain one of the city's symbols.

IGREJA DE SANTO ANTÓNIO AND MUSEU ANTONIANO

Largo S. António da Sé ☎ 218 860 447. Tram #28. MAP P.40–41, POCKET MAP E12

The small eighteenth-century church of **Santo António** (open daily) is said to have been built on the spot where the city's most popular saint was born as Fernando Bulhões; after his death in Italy in 1231 he became known as Saint Anthony of Padua. The tiny neighbouring **museum** (Tues–Sun 10am–1pm & 2–6pm; free) chronicles the saint's life, including his enviable skill at fixing marriages, though only devotees will find interest in the statues and endless images.

CASA DOS BICOS

Rua dos Bacalhoeiros ☎ 218 810 900. Entry varies. MAP P.40–41, POCKET MAP F13

The Casa dos Bicos means the "House of Points", and its curious walls – set with diamond-shaped stones – give an idea of the richness of pre-1755 Lisbon. It was built in 1523 for the son of the Viceroy of India, though only the facade of the original building survived the earthquake. It is now owned by the Saramargo organisation (Ⓦ www.josesaramago.org) who use the venue for recitals and exhibitions dedicated to the Nobel Prize for Literature winning Portuguese author José Saramago who died in 2010.

Tram #25 to Prazeres

The open area to the south of the Casa dos Bicos is the terminus for another of Lisbon's classic tram rides, the #25 (Mon–Fri every 15 mins from 7am–9pm), which sees far fewer tourists than tram #28 (see p.45) but takes almost as picturesque a route. From here it trundles along the riverfront and up through Lapa and Estrela to the suburb of Prazeres, best known as the site of one of Lisbon's largest cemeteries. You can stroll round the enormous plot where family tombs are movingly adorned with trinkets

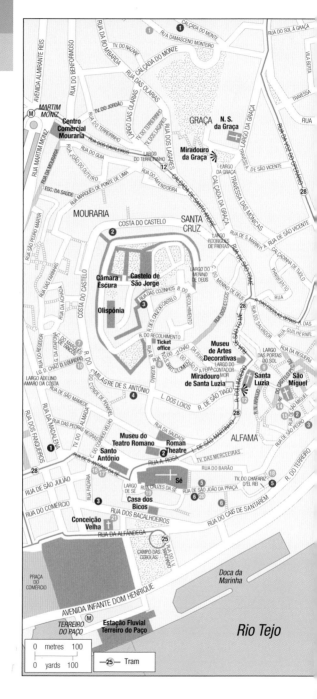

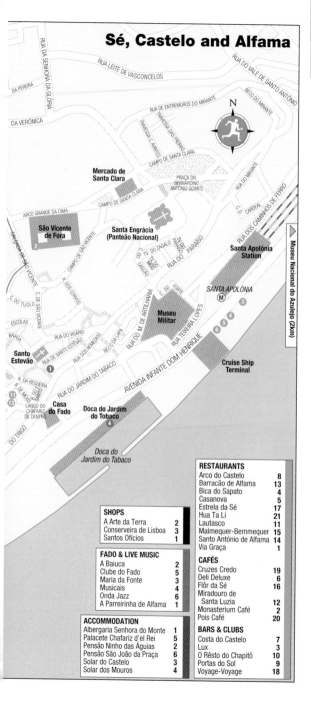

Sé, Castelo and Alfama

N

RUA DA SENHORA DA GLÓRIA
DA PEREIRA
DA VERÓNICA

RUA LEITE DE VASCONCELOS
RUA DO VALE DE SANTO ANTÓNIO
RUA DE ENTREMUROS DO MIRANTE
BECO DO MIRANTE
TRAVESSA C. ANTES DE FREIRAS
CAMPO DE SANTA CLARA
RUA DO MIRANTE

Mercado de Santa Clara
PRAÇA DR. BERNARDINO ANTÓNIO GOMES
CAMPO DE SANTA CLARA

ARCO GRANDE DA CIMA
CALÇADA DE SÃO VICENTE

São Vicente de Fora
Santa Engrácia (Panteão Nacional)
CAMPO DE SÃO VICENTE
RUA DOS CAMINHOS DE FERRO

Santa Apolónia Station
C. DO FORTE
TV. DO ZAGALO
RUA DO PARAÍSO
CASCAO
CARDEAL

C. DO TIJOLO
C. DE SÃO VICENTE
R. DOS CORVOS
RUA DO VIGÁRIO

ESCOLAS
BRAGA
RUA DE SANTO ESTÊVÃO
RUA DOS REMÉDIOS
BECO DA LIRA
RUA DA M. DE ARTILHARIA

SANTA APOLÓNIA
Ⓜ
Museu Militar
RUA TEIXEIRA LOPES

Santo Estevão
R. DA REGUEIRA
R. DE MEIO
LARGO DO CHAFARIZ DE DENTRO
Casa do Fado
RUA DO JARDIM DO TABACO
AVENIDA INFANTE DOM HENRIQUE

Cruise Ship Terminal

DO TRIGO
Doca do Jardim do Tobaco

Doca do Jardim do Tabaco

▷ Museu Nacional do Azulejo (2km)

RESTAURANTS

Arco do Castelo	8
Barracão de Alfama	13
Bica do Sapato	4
Casanova	5
Estrela da Sé	17
Hua Ta Li	21
Lautasco	11
Malmequer-Bemmequer	15
Santo António de Alfama	14
Via Graça	1

SHOPS

A Arte da Terra	2
Conserveira de Lisboa	3
Santos Ofícios	1

CAFÉS

Cruzes Credo	19
Deli Deluxe	6
Flôr da Sé	16
Miradouro de Santa Luzia	12
Monasterium Café	2
Pois Café	20

FADO & LIVE MUSIC

A Baiuca	2
Clube do Fado	5
Maria da Fonte	3
Musicais	4
Onda Jazz	6
A Parreirinha de Alfama	1

BARS & CLUBS

Costa do Castelo	7
Lux	3
O Rêsto do Chapitô	10
Portas do Sol	9
Voyage-Voyage	18

ACCOMMODATION

Albergaria Senhora do Monte	1
Palacete Chafariz d'el Rei	5
Pensão Ninho das Águias	2
Pensão São João da Praça	6
Solar do Castelo	3
Solar dos Mouros	4

MUSEU DO TEATRO ROMANO

Entrance on Patio de Aljube 5 ☎ 218 820 320, ⓦ www.museu-teatroromano.net. Tues–Sun 10am–1pm & 2–6pm. Free. Tram #28. MAP P.40-41, POCKET MAP F12

The Museu do Teatro Romano displays a wealth of Roman coins, spoons and fragments of pots, statues and columns excavated from the ruins of a Roman theatre, dating from 57 AD, which are fenced off just north of Rua Augusto Rosa. Roman Lisbon – Olisipo – became the administrative capital of Lusitania, the western part of Iberia, under Julius Caesar in 60 BC, and the theatre shows the wealth that quickly grew thanks to its fish-preserving industries.

MIRADOURO DE SANTA LUZIA

MAP P.40-41, POCKET MAP F12

The church of Santa Luzia marks the entry to the Miradouro de Santa Luzia, a spectacular viewpoint where elderly Lisboetas play cards and tourists gather to take in the sweeping views across the Alfama and the river beyond.

MUSEU DE ARTES DECORATIVAS

Largo das Portas do Sol 2 ☎ 218 814 600, ⓦ www.fress.pt. Mon & Wed–Sun 10am–5pm. €4. Tram #28. MAP P.40-41, POCKET MAP F11

Set in the seventeenth-century Azurara Palace, this fascinating museum contains some of the best examples of sixteenth- to eighteenth-century applied art in the country. Founded by a wealthy banker and donated to the nation in 1953, the museum boasts unique pieces of furniture, major collections of gold, silver and porcelain, magnificent paintings and textiles. The rambling building covers five floors, set around a stairway decorated with spectacular azulejos. Highlights include a stunning sixteenth-century tapestry depicting a parade of giraffes, beautiful carpets from Arraiolos in the Alentejo district, and oriental-influenced quilts that were all the rage during the seventeenth and eighteenth centuries. The museum also has a small café with a patio garden.

CASTELO DE SÃO JORGE

☎ 218 800 620, ⓦ www.castelosaojorge .pt. Daily: March–Oct 9am–9pm; Nov–Feb 9am–6pm. €7.50 includes visit to Câmara Escura and Olisipónia. Bus #37 from Praça da Figueira. MAP P.40-41, POCKET MAP F11

Reached by a confusing but well-signposted series of twisting roads, the Castelo de São Jorge is perhaps the most spectacular building in Lisbon, as much because of its position as anything else. Now Lisbon's most-visited tourist site, the castle's was once the heart of a walled city that spread downhill as far as the river. The original Moorish castle on this site was besieged in 1147 by a particularly ruthless gang of Crusaders who, together with King Alfonso I of Portugal, conquered Lisbon after some

four hundred years of Moorish rule. Badly damaged during the seige, its fortifications were rebuilt. From the fourteenth century, Portuguese kings took up residence in the old Moorish palace, or Alcáçova, within the walls, but by the early sixteenth century they had moved to the new royal palace on Praça do Comércio. Subsequently, the castle was used as a prison and then as an army barracks until the 1920s. The walls were partly renovated by Salazar in the 1930s and further restored for the Expo 98. A series of gardens, walkways and **viewpoints** hidden within the old Moorish walls makes this an enjoyable place in which to wander about for a couple of hours, with spectacular views over the city from its ramparts and towers.

CÂMARA ESCURA

Castelo de São Jorge. Weather permitting daily: 10am–5pm. MAP P.40-41, POCKET MAP F11

One of the castle towers, the Tower of Ulysses, now holds a kind of periscope which projects sights from around the city onto a white disk with commentary in English. Unless you like being holed up in dark chambers with up to fifteen other people, though, you may prefer to see the view in the open air.

THE ALCÁÇOVA AND OLISIPÓNIA

Castelo de São Jorge. Daily: March–Oct 10am–8pm; Nov–Feb 9am–5.30pm. MAP P.40-41, POCKET MAP F11

Only a much-restored shell remains of the old Moorish Alcáçova. This now houses Olisipónia, a multimedia history of Lisbon shown in three underground chambers. Portable headsets provide a 35-minute commentary on aspects of Lisbon's development; although the presentations overlap somewhat and gloss over a few of Lisbon's less savoury chapters, such as slavery and the Inquisition, they are a useful introduction to the city.

SANTA CRUZ AND MOURARIA

Castelo de São Jorge. MAP P.40-41, POCKET MAP F11

Crammed within the castle's outer walls is the tiny medieval quarter of Santa Cruz. This remains a village in its own right, with its own school, bathhouse and church. Leaving Santa Cruz, a tiny arch at the end of Rua do Chão da Feira leads through to Rua dos Cegos and down to Largo Rodrigues de Freitas, which marks the eastern edge of Mouraria, the district to which the Moors were relegated after the siege of Lisbon – hence the name. Today Mouraria is an atmospheric residential area with some of the city's best African restaurants, especially around Largo de São Cristóvão.

SANTA ENGRÁCIA

MIRADOURO DA GRAÇA

MAP P.40–41, POCKET MAP F10

The Miradouro da Graça
provides superb views over
Lisbon and the castle. To reach
it take Tram #28 (see p.45)
to the broad Largo da Graça.
From here, head past Nossa
Senhora da Graça – a church
which partly dates from 1271,
making it one of the oldest
in the city – to the viewpoint
which also has a small kiosk
café-bar.

SÃO VICENTE DE FORA

Tues–Sun 10am–6pm. Church free, monastery
€4. Tram #28. MAP P.40–41, POCKET MAP G11

The church of São Vicente de
Fora stands as a reminder of the
extent of the sixteenth-century
city; its name means "Saint
Vincent of the Outside". It was
built during the years of Spanish
rule by Philip II's Italian architect, Felipe Terzi (1582–1629);
its geometric facade was an
important Renaissance innova-
tion. Of more interest is the
adjoining monastery. Through
the beautiful cloisters, decorated
with azulejos representing
scenes from Portugal's history,
you can visit the old monastic
refectory, which since 1855 has

formed the pantheon of the
Bragança dynasty. Here, in more
or less complete sequence, are
the **tombs** of all the Portuguese kings from João IV, who
restored the monarchy in 1640,
to Manuel II, the last Portuguese
monarch who died in exile in
England in 1932. Among them
is Catherine of Bragança, the
widow of England's Charles II,
who is credited with introducing
the concept of "teatime" to the
British. If you have energy,
climb to the roof for spectacular
views out over the city. There's
also a lovely café by the entrance
if you do fancy a cup of tea.

FEIRA DA LADRA

Tues and Sat 9am–around 3pm. Tram #28.
MAP P.40–41, POCKET MAP H10

The broad, leafy square of
Campo de Santa Clara is home
to the twice-weekly Feira da
Ladra ("Thieves' Market"),
Lisbon's main flea market. It's
not the world's greatest market,
but it does turn up some
interesting things, like oddities
from the former African
colonies and old Portuguese
prints. Out-and-out junk –
from broken alarm clocks to
old postcards – is spread on the

ground above Santa Engrácia, with cheap clothes, CDs and half-genuine antiques at the top end of the *feira*. The covered *mercado* (market) building has a fine array of fresh fruit and vegetables.

SANTA ENGRÁCIA

Campo de Santa Clara. Tues–Sun: May–Oct 10am–6pm; Nov–April 10am–5pm. €3. Tram #28. MAP P.40–41, POCKET MAP H10

The white dome of Santa Engrácia makes it the loftiest church in the city, and it has become synonymous with unfinished work – begun in 1682, it was only completed in 1966. It is now the **Panteão Nacional**, housing the tombs of eminent Portuguese figures, including writer Almeida Garrett (1799–1854) and Amália Rodrigues (1920–99), Portugal's most famous fado singer. You can take the stairs up to the terrace, from where there are great views over eastern Lisbon.

THE ALFAMA

MAP P.40–41, POCKET MAP G12

In Moorish times, the Alfama was the grandest part of the city, but as Lisbon expanded, the new Christian nobility moved out, leaving it to the local fishing community. None of today's houses dates from before the Christian

IGREJA DE SÃO MIGUEL, ALFAMA

Reconquest, but you'll notice a kasbah-like layout. Although an increasing number of fado restaurants are moving in, the quarter retains a quiet, village-like quality. Life continues much as it has done for years in the labyrinthine streets, with people buying groceries and fish from hole-in-the-wall stores and householders stoking small outdoor charcoal grills. Half the fun of exploring here is getting lost, but at some point head for Rua de São Miguel – off which run some of the most interesting *becos* (alleys) – and for the parallel street Rua de São Pedro, where *varinas* (fishwives) sell the catch of the day from tiny stalls.

Tram #28

The picture-book tram #28 is one of the city's greatest rides, though its popularity is such that there are usually queues to get on and standing room only is more than likely. Built in England in the early twentieth century, the trams are all polished wood and chrome but give a distinctly rough ride up and down Lisbon's steepest streets, at times coming so close to shops that you could almost take a can of sardines off the shelves. From Graça, the tram plunges down through Alfama to the Baixa and up to Prazeres, to the west of the centre. Take care of belongings as pickpockets also enjoy the ride.

CASA DO FADO E DA GUITARRA PORTUGUESA

Largo do Chafariz de Dentro ☎ 218 823 470, Ⓦ www.museudofado.pt. Tues–Sun 10am–6pm. €5. MAP P.40-41, POCKET MAP G12

Set in the renovated Recinto da Praia, a former water cistern and bathhouse, the Casa do Fado e da Guitarra Portuguesa provides an excellent introduction to this quintessentially Portuguese art form (for more on fado see the box, p.51). The museum details the history of fado and its importance to the Portuguese people; its shop stocks a great selection of CDs. A series of rooms in the museum contains wax models, photographs, famous paintings of fado scenes and descriptions of the leading singers. It also traces the history of the Portuguese guitar, an essential element of the fado performance. Interactive displays allow you to listen to the different types of fado (Lisbon has its own kind, differing from that of the northern city of Coimbra), varying from mournful to positively racy.

TILE DETAIL, MUSEU NACIONAL DO AZULEJO

DOCA DO JARDIM DO TOBACO

Bus #28, 35 or 794 from Praça do Comércio. MAP P.40-41, POCKET MAP H12

Next to Lisbon's main cruise ship terminal lies the dockland development of the Doca do Jardim do Tobaco. Its name, "Tobacco Garden Dock", refers to its previous role as the city's main depot for storing tobacco. Facing one of the broadest sections of the Rio Tejo, it's a great place for a sunset drink or an evening meal, its restaurants and bars attracting a well-to-do crowd.

MUSEU NACIONAL DO AZULEJO

Rua da Madre de Deus 4 ☎ 218 103 340, Ⓦ www.mnazulejo.imc-ip.pt. Tues 2–6pm, Wed–Sun 10am–6pm. €5, free Sun 10am–2pm. Bus #794 from Praça do Comércio/Santa Apolónia. MAP P.40-41, POCKET MAP M5

The Museu Nacional do Azulejo (tile museum) traces the development of Portuguese azulejo tiles from fifteenth-century Moorish styles to the present day, with each room representing a different period. Diverse styles range from seventeenth-century portraits of the English King Charles II with his Portuguese wife, Catherine of Bragança, to the 1720 satirical panel depicting a man being given an injection in his bottom. The museum is inside the church Madre de Deus, whose eighteenth-century tiled scenes of St Anthony are among the best in the city. Many of the rooms are housed round the church's cloisters – look for the spire in one corner of the main cloister, itself completely tiled. The highlight upstairs is Portugal's longest azulejo – a wonderfully detailed 40-metre panorama of Lisbon, completed in around 1738. The museum also has a good café-restaurant and shop.

some attractive ceramics, rugs, embroidery, baskets and toys.

Restaurants

ARCO DO CASTELO

Rua do Chão da Feira 25 ☎ 218 876 598. Mon–Sat noon–midnight. MAP P.40-41, POCKET MAP F12

Cheerful place just below the entrance to the castle, specializing in moderately priced Goan dishes – choose from tempting shrimp curry, Indian sausage or spicy seafood. Mains are from €9.

BARRACÃO DE ALFAMA

Rua de S. Pedro 16 ☎ 218 866 359. Daily 11am–midnight. MAP P.40-41, POCKET MAP G12

An unpretentious tiled local tasca popular with locals, with non-touristy prices: you can have a full meal here for under €15. Portions are generous with fine fish and grills from under €8. There are a few outdoor tables at the back in summer.

BICA DO SAPATO

Avda Infante Dom Henrique, Armazém B, Cais da Pedra à Bica do Sapato ☎ 218 810 320. Mon 8pm–midnight, Tues–Sat 12.30pm–midnight, Sun 11.30am–3.30pm. MAP P.40-41, POCKET MAP M6

This stylish yet informal warehouse conversion has mirrored walls to reflect the crisp Tejo vistas. There's an outside terrace, too. The chef creates what he calls a "laboratory of Portuguese ingredients", including hare with rice and a fabulous "crustacean mix" of crabs and tiger prawns as well as pasta and sushi. Satisfied guests have included Pedro Almodóvar, Catherine Deneuve and architect Frank Gehry, though its prices (mains €13–20) are affordable to mere mortals.

Shops

A ARTE DA TERRA

Rua de Augusto Rosa 40 Mon–Sat 11am–8pm, Sun 11am–6pm. MAP P.40-41, POCKET MAP F12.

Housed in historic stables – with some of the handicrafts displayed in the stone horse troughs – this is a beautiful space with a range of local arts and crafts, from jewellery and cork products to postcards, preserves and souvenirs.

CONSERVEIRA DE LISBOA

Rua dos Bacalhoeiras 34. Mon–Fri 9am–7pm, Sat 9.30am–1pm. MAP P.40-41, POCKET MAP E13

Wall-to-wall tin cans stuffed into wooden cabinets make this colourful 1930s shop a bizarre but intriguing place to stock up on tinned sardines, squid, salmon, mussels and just about any other sea beast you can think of.

SANTOS OFÍCIOS

Rua da Madalena 87. Mon–Sat 10am–8pm. MAP P.40-41, POCKET MAP E12

Small shop crammed with a somewhat touristy collection of regional crafts, but including

CASANOVA

Avda Infante Dom Henrique, Loja 7 Armazém
B, Cais da Pedra à Bica do Sapato ☎ 218
877 532. Daily 12.30pm–1.30am. MAP P.40–41,
POCKET MAP M6

If *Bica do Sapato* is beyond
your budget, the more
modestly priced *Casanova* next
door offers pizza, pasta and
crostini accompanied by similar
views from its outside terrace.
It's phenomenally popular and
you can't book, so turn up
early. Expect to pay around €15
for a meal and drink.

ESTRELA DA SÉ

Largo S. António da Sé 4 ☎ 218 870 455.
Mon–Fri 9am–9pm, Sat 9am–2pm. MAP P.40–41,
POCKET MAP E12

Beautiful azulejo-covered
restaurant near the Sé, serving
inexpensive and tasty dishes
like *alheira* (chicken sausage),
salmon and Spanish-style tapas.
Its wooden booths – perfect for
discreet trysts – date from the
nineteenth century.

HUA TA LI

Rua dos Bacalhoeiros 109–115 ☎ 218 879
170. Daily noon–3.30pm & 6.30–11pm. MAP
P.40–41, POCKET MAP E13

Great value Chinese restaurant
(mains from €6), very popular
for Sunday lunch, when it
heaves with diners (so it's
best to book). Seafood scores
highly; try the squid chop suey.
It's also good for vegetarians.

LAUTASCO

Beco do Azinhal 7 ☎ 218 860 173. Mon–Sat
10am–3pm & 9–10.30pm; closed Dec. MAP
P.40–41, POCKET MAP G12

Tucked just off the Largo do
Chafariz de Dentro, in a picturesque Alfama courtyard; by day
a shady retreat, by night
a magical, fairy-lit oasis.
Multilingual menus and higher
than usual prices (mains
from around €12) suggest a

DELI DELUXE

largely tourist clientele but
it's a great spot for *borrego*
(lamb), *tamboril* (monkfish) or
cataplanas (stews). Bookings
are advised.

MALMEQUER-BEMMEQUER

Rua de São Miguel 23–25 ☎ 218 876 535.
Wed–Sun 12.30–3.30pm & 7.30–10.30pm,
Tues 7.30–10.30pm; closed last week in Oct.
MAP P.40–41, POCKET MAP G12

Cheerily decorated and moderately priced place, overseen by
a friendly owner. Grilled meat
and fish dishes dominate the
menu (try the *salmão no carvão*
– charcoal-grilled salmon), or
eat from the daily changing
tourist menu – mains €7–9.

SANTO ANTÓNIO DE ALFAMA

Beco de São Miguel 7 ☎ 218 881 328 or 218
881 329. Daily 12.30pm–2am. MAP P.40–41,
POCKET MAP G12

With a lovely outdoor terrace
shaded by vines, this is one of
the nicest restaurant-bars in
the Alfama; it's off Rua de São
Miguel; book to guarantee a
table. There's a very long list of
expensive wines; pasta and fish
dishes from €13 or a range of
less pricey tapas from €7.

VIA GRAÇA

Rua Damasceno Monteiro 9b ☎ 218 870 830.
Mon–Fri 12.30–3pm & 7.30–11pm, Sat & Sun
7.30–11pm. MAP P.40–41, POCKET MAP K5

Tucked away below the
Miradouro da Graça (take a left
after Largo da Graça becomes
Rua da Graça), this smart and
expensive restaurant in an
unattractive modern building is
a whole lot better on the inside,
from where you can soak up
the stunning panoramas of
Lisbon. Specialities include
roast goat with rice and game
cataplana from around €20–25.

Cafés

CRUZES CREDO

Rua Cruzes da Sé 29 ☎ 218 822 296. Daily
10am–2am. Map p.40–41, POCKET MAP F12.

This fashionable little café has a
jazzy ambience and serves tasty
petiscos snacks including some
unusual (for these parts) dishes
such as bruschetta, humous
and burgers (€5–7). It's also a
tranquil spot for a drink.

DELI DELUXE

Avda Infante Dom Henrique, Armazem
B, Loja 8. Tues–Fri noon–midnight, Sat
10am–midnight, Sun 10am–8pm. MAP P.40–41,
POCKET MAP M6

A modern deli with delectable
cheeses, cured meats and
preserves, though the riverside
café at the back is even more
appealing. Grab a seat outdoors
and enjoy the range of goodies
from croissants to speciality
teas, , salads and cocktails.

FLÔR DA SÉ

Largo da Sé. Mon–Sat 7am–8pm. MAP P.40–41,
POCKET MAP E12

Conveniently near the
cathedral, this *pastelaria* has a
counter packed with pastries
and savouries. Tables are set
out beneath azulejos depicting
Santo António. It also does
decent, inexpensive lunches.

MIRADOURO DE SANTA LUZIA

Miradouro de Santa Luzia. Daily 9am–11pm.
MAP P.40–41, POCKET MAP F12

Hilltop suntrap just below the
viewpoint of the same name.
Drinks and meals are slightly
pricey (around €11) but you
pay for the views, which are
fabulous.

MONASTERIUM CAFÉ

Igreja São Vicente de Fora, Calçada de
São Vicente ☎ 218 885 652. Tues–Sun
10am–6pm. MAP P.40–41, POCKET MAP G11

The São Vicente monastery
café boasts comfortable indoor
seating and a tranquil patio, a
lovely spot for a drink or light
lunch.

POIS CAFÉ

Rua São João da Praça 93–95. Tues–Sun
11am–8pm. MAP P.40–41, POCKET MAP F12

With its big comfy sofas and
laid-back ambience, this high,
arched ceiling café is a must.
There's a friendly, young
crowd, books to dip into, light
meals and home-made snacks,
including a great *apfelstrudel*.

POIS CAFÉ

Bars and clubs

COSTA DO CASTELO

Calçada do Marquês de Tancos 1b ☎ 218 884 636. Mon–Sat noon–midnight. MAP P.40–41, POCKET MAP E11

Terrace-bar/restaurant with a long list of cocktails and mid-priced pasta and fish dishes. Occasional live music and events, usually at weekends.

LUX

Armazéns A, Cais da Pedra a Santa Apolónia ⓦ www.luxfragil.com. Tues–Sun midnight–6am. MAP P.40–41, POCKET MAP M6

This converted former meat warehouse has become one of Europe's most fashion-able spaces, attracting A-list visitors such as Prince and Cameron Diaz. Part-owned by actor John Malkovich, it was the first place to venture into the docks opposite Santa Apolónia station. There's a rooftop terrace with amazing views, various bars, projection screens, a frenzied downstairs dancefloor, and music from pop and trance to jazz and dance. The club is also increas-ingly on the circuit for touring bands.

PORTAS DO SOL

Largo Portas do Sol ☎ 218 851 299, ⓦ www.portasdosol.biz. Mon–Thurs 10am–midnight, Fri–Sat 1am–2am. MAP P.40–41, POCKET MAP G12

As you might guess from the name, this hip spot is an obligatory venue for anyone into sunsets. Hiding under the lip of the road, it's a chic indoor space, though most people head for the outside seats on the giant terrace with grandstand views over the Alfama. Pricey drinks, coffees and cocktails, but worth it. DJs on Fridays and Saturdays.

O RÊSTO DO CHAPITÔ

Costa do Castelo 7 ☎ 218 867 734, ⓦ www.chapito.org. Restaurant daily noon–6pm & 7.30–midnight. Bar daily noon–1.30am. MAP P.40–41, POCKET MAP E12

Multipurpose venue incorpo-rating a theatre, circus school, restaurant and tapas bar. The restaurant is in an upstairs dining room, reached via a spiral staircase, and serves a range of menus with mains such as black pork with ginger and mushroom risotto from €16. The outdoor esplanade commands terrific views over Alfama and most people come here to drink and take in the view. Check the website for live music, films and readings.

VOYAGE-VOYAGE

Trav. do Chafariz d'El Rei 8 ☎ 211 955 434. Wed–Thurs 8pm–2am, Fri–Sat 8pm–4am, Sun 11am–8pm. MAP P.40–41, POCKET MAP G12

This striking eastern-inspired bar combines oriental decor with Parisian chic; its French owner rustles up superb cocktails and snacks. Weekend DJ sessions and Sunday brunches see it at its liveliest.

O RÊSTO DO CHAPITÔ

Fado and live music

A BAIUCA

Rua de São Miguel 20 ☎ 218 867 284. Thurs–Mon 7.30–11pm. MAP P.40-41, POCKET MAP G12

Nightly fado is performed in this great little tiled *tasca* which serves decent fresh fish and grills from €15. Reservations advised.

CLUBE DO FADO

Rua de São João da Praça 94 ☎ 218 852 704, Ⓦ www.clube-de-fado.com. Daily 8pm–2am. MAP P.40-41, POCKET MAP F12

Intimate and homely fado club with stone pillars, an old well as a decorative feature, and a mainly local clientele. It attracts small-time performers, up-and-coming talent and the occasional big name. Expect to pay €50 or so including food.

MARIA DA FONTE

Rua de São Pedro 5a ☎ 963 814 324. Tues–Sun 8pm–2am. MAP P.40-41, POCKET MAP G12

Tiny, intimate tiled *casa do fado* with good-value fish dishes. The speciality is *bife na pedra* (steak cooked on a hot stone).

Live fado from 8pm on most nights, when average prices are €25–30 a head.

MUSICAIS

Doca do Jardim do Tobaco Pavilhão A/B Ⓦ www.musicaisbar.com. Daily 3pm–2am. MAP P.40-41, POCKET MAP H12

Dockside bar with fine river views and live music most nights from 11.30pm, usually from Thursday to Sunday. Sounds range from flamenco and folk to occasional rock.

ONDA JAZZ

Arco de Jesus 7 ☎ 218 883 242, Ⓦ www .ondajazz.com Tues–Sat 8pm–2am. MAP P.40-41, POCKET MAP F12

One of Lisbon's best jazz clubs, with regular top-name acts as well as local musicians. Wednesday night jamming sessions, with live shows nightly from 10.30pm.

A PARREIRINHA DE ALFAMA

Beco do Espírito Santo 1 ☎ 218 868 209. Daily 8pm–3am. MAP P.40-41, POCKET MAP G12

One of the best fado venues owned by famous fado singer Argentina Santos, just off Largo do Chafariz de Dentro, often attracting leading stars and an enthusiastic local clientele. Reservations are advised when the big names appear.

Fado

Fado (literally "fate") is often described as a kind of Portuguese blues. Popular themes are love, death, bullfighting and indeed fate itself. It is believed to derive from music that was popular with eighteenth-century immigrants from Portugal's colonies who first settled in Alfama. Famous singers like Maria Severa and Amália Rodrigues grew up in Alfama, which since the 1930s has hosted some of the city's most authentic fado houses – stroll around after 8pm and you'll hear magical sounds emanating from various venues, or better still, enjoy a meal at one of the places we list above. The big contemporary name is Mariza, who grew up in neighbouring Mouraria. Other singers to look out for (though unlikely to appear in small venues) are Mizia, Carminho, Helder Moutinho, Carlos do Carmo, Maria da Fé and Cristina Branco.

Chiado and Cais do Sodré

The well-to-do district of Chiado (pronounced she-ar-doo) is famed for its smart shops and cafés, along with the city's main museum for contemporary arts. Down on the waterfront, Cais do Sodré (pronounced kaiysh doo soodray) is a down-at-heel suburb. Many of its waterfront warehouses have been converted into upmarket cafés and restaurants and by day, in particular, a stroll along its characterful riverfront is very enjoyable. Nearby Mercado da Ribeira, Lisbon's main market, is also big on atmosphere, as is the hillside Bica district, which is served by another of the city's classic funicular street lifts – Elevador da Bica. Cais do Sodré is also where you can catch ferries across the Tejo to the little port of Cacilhas which not only has some great seafood restaurants with views over Lisbon, but it is also the bus terminus for some of the region's best beaches and for the spectacular Cristo Rei statue of Christ.

RUA GARRETT

MAP P.53, POCKET MAP C12

Chiado's most famous street, Rua Garrett, is where you'll find some of the oldest shops and cafés in the city, including *A Brasileira* (see p.58). Beggars usually mark the nearby entrance to the **Igreja dos Mártires** (Church of the Martyrs), named after the English Crusaders who were killed during the siege of Lisbon. Some of the area's best shops can also be found in nearby Rua do Carmo. This was the heart of the area that was greatly damaged by a fire in 1988, although the original *belle époque* atmosphere has since been superbly recreated under the direction of eminent Portuguese architect Álvaro Siza Vieira.

RUA GARRETT

TEATRO NACIONAL DE SÃO CARLOS

Rua Serpa Pinto 9 213 253 000, www.saocarlos.pt. Café daily from 10am. MAP ABOVE, POCKET MAP C13.

Lisbon's main opera house, the Teatro Nacional de São Carlos, was built shortly after the original Lisbon opera house on Praça do Comércio was destroyed in the Great Earthquake. Heavily influenced by the leading Italian opera houses, it has a sumptuous Rococo interior, but you can only see it during performances. You can enjoy the theatre's café at other times, with pleasant outside tables surrounded by olive trees.

Fernando Pessoa

Café A Brasileira is marked by a bronze statue of Fernando Pessoa (1888–1935), Portugal's greatest contemporary poet and a leading figure of twentieth century modernism. Born in Lisbon, Pessoa grew up in South Africa before returning to Portugal in 1905 to work as a translator. He spent much of his time composing poems in Lisbon's cafés. Many of his works are about identity – he wrote under various alter egos or "heteronyms", each with their own personality and style. The most famous are Alberto Caeiro, Ricardo Reis and Alvaro de Campos, though his most famous work is the Book of Disquiet written under the heteronym Bernardo Soares. The partly autobiographical work is full of extraordinary philosophical ruminations that have established his reputation as a leading existentialist artist.

MUSEU DO CHIADO

Rua Serpa Pinto 4 ☎ 213 432 148, ⓦ www
.museudochiado-ipmuseus.pt. Tues–Sun
10am–6pm. €4, free Sun 10am–2pm. MAP P.53,
POCKET MAP C13

The Museu do Chiado traces
the history of art from
Romanticism to Modernism.
It is housed in a stylish
building with a pleasant
courtyard café and rooftop
terrace, constructed around
a nineteenth-century biscuit
factory. Within the gallery's
permanent collection are
works by some of Portugal's
most influential artists since
the nineteenth century, along
with foreign artists influenced
by Portugal including Rodin.
Highlights include Almada
Negreiros' 1920s panels from
the old São Carlos cinema,
showing Felix the Cat; a
beautiful sculpture, *A Viúva*
(*The Widow*), by António
Teixeira Lopes; and some
evocative early twentieth-
century Lisbon scenes by
watercolourist Carlos Botelho.
There are also frequent temporary exhibitions.

A VIÚVA, MUSEU DO CHIADO

MIRADOURO DE SANTA CATARINA

Tram #28. MAP P.53, POCKET MAP A12

Set on the cusp of a hill high
above the river, the railed
Miradouro de Santa Catarina
has spectacular views. Here, in
the shadow of the statue of the
Adamastor – a mythical beast
from Luís de Camões's *Lusiads*
– a mixture of oddballs and
New Age types often collects
around an alluring drinks kiosk
(daily 10am–dusk, weather
permitting), which has a few
outdoor tables.

ELEVADOR DA BICA

Entrance on Rua de São Paulo. Mon–Sat
7am–9pm, Sun 9am–9pm. €3.50 return. MAP
P.53, POCKET MAP B13

With its entrance tucked into
an arch on Rua de São Paulo,
the Elevador da Bica is one of
the city's most atmospheric
funicular railways. Built in
1892 – and originally powered
by water counterweights, but
now electrically operated – the
elevador leads up towards
the Bairro Alto, via a steep
residential street. Take time to
explore the steep side streets of
the Bica neighbourhood, too, a
warren of characterful houses,
little shops and fine local
restaurants.

MERCADO DA RIBEIRA

Main entrance on Rua Dom Luís I. ⓦ www
.espacoribeira.pt. Main market Tues–Sat
5am–2pm. MAP P.53, POCKET MAP B13

The Mercado da Ribeira is
Lisbon's most historic market.
Built originally on the site of
an old fort at the end of the
nineteenth century, the current
structure dates only from 1930.
The market downstairs has
an impressive array of fresh
fish, fruit and vegetables, with
a separate, aromatic flower
section (open until 7pm). In
the past it was traditional for

Lisboetas to enjoy a *cacau da Ribeira* (cocoa) here after a night out on the town, and the local council recently decided to renovate the market building in an attempt to restore this social function. As a result, the upper level now hosts Wednesday to Sunday live music ranging from jazz to folk, performed either on a central stage or in the pub-like *RibeirArte Café* in the upper level. On Sundays there is a morning collectors' market.

CACILHAS AND ALMADA

MAP P.53, POCKET MAP J8

The short, blustery ferry ride from Lisbon's Cais do Sodré over the Tejo to Cacilhas is great fun and grants wonderful views of the city. Cacilhas is little more than a bustling bus and ferry terminal with a pretty church, surrounded by lively stalls and cafés, but is well known for its seafood restaurants. You can also visit the wooden-hulled, fifty-gun **Dom Fernando II e Glória frigate** (📞917 841 149; Tues–Sun 10am–5pm; €3) on Largo Alfredo Diniz. Built in India in 1843, it's now a museum showing what life at sea was like in the mid-nineteenth century. A good riverside walk is to head west towards the bridge along the waterfront. It's around fifteen minutes' walk to the **Elevador Panorâmico da Boca do Vento** (daily 8am–midnight; €2 return), a sleek lift that whisks you 30m up the cliff face to the attractive old

CRISTO REI

part of Almada, giving fantastic views over the river and city.

CRISTO REI

Bus #101 from outside the Cacilhas ferry terminal; Lift open daily: June–Sept 9.30am–6.30pm; Oct–May 9.30am–6.15pm; €5 return; 🌐 www.cristorei.pt. MAP P.53, POCKET MAP H9

On the heights above Almada stand the outstretched arms of Cristo Rei, built in 1959 as a pilgrimage site to grace Portugal's non-participation in World War II. A lift at the statue shuttles you a further 80m up to a dramatic viewing platform, from where, on a clear day, you can catch a glimpse of the glistening roof of the Pena palace at Sintra.

Travel to Cacilhas and beyond

Cais do Sodré is the main departure point for ferries over the Tejo to the largely industrial suburbs to the south. Ferries to Cacilhas (🌐 www.transtejo.pt) every 15min, 5.40am–2.30am; €1.10 single) dock by a bus and tram depot from where buses run to Costa da Caparica (see p.125).

Shops

ANA SALAZAR

Rua do Carmo 87. Mon–Sat 10am–7pm.
MAP P.53, POCKET MAP D11

One of Lisbon's best-known names for modern and individual designer clothes for men and women, together with bags and belts.

ARMAZÉNS DO CHIADO

Rua do Carmo 2. Daily 10am–10pm, restaurants until 11pm. MAP P.53, POCKET MAP D12

This swish shopping centre sits on six floors above metro Baixa-Chiado in a structure that has risen from the ashes of the Chiado fire, though it retains its traditional facade. Various shops include branches of Massimo Duti (women), Sportzone, Bodyshop and the classy toy shop Imaginarium. The top floor has a series of cafés and restaurants, including Brazilian chain *Chimarrão*, most offering great views.

FÁBRICA SANT'ANNA

Rua do Alecrim 95. Mon–Fri 9.30am–7pm, Sat 10am–2pm. MAP P.53, POCKET MAP C13

If you're interested in Portuguese azulejos, check out this factory shop, founded in 1741, which sells copies of traditional designs and a great range of ceramics.

LIVRARIA BERTRAND

Rua Garrett 73. Mon–Thurs 9am–8pm, Fri & Sat 9am–10pm, Sun 2–10pm. MAP P.53, POCKET MAP C12

Portugal's oldest bookshop, founded in 1773 and once the meeting place for Lisbon's literary set. Offering novels in English and a range of foreign magazines, it's also a good place to find English translations of Portuguese writers including Fernando Pessoa.

STORYTAILORS

LUVARIA ULISSES

Rua do Carmo 87a. Mon–Sat 10am–7pm.
MAP P.53, POCKET MAP D11

The superb, ornately carved wooden doorway leads you into a minuscule glove shop, with hand-wear to suit all tastes tucked into rows of boxes.

STORYTAILORS

Calçada do Ferragial 8. Tues–Sat noon–8pm.
MAP P.53, POCKET MAP C13

Set in a suitably stylish bare-brick eighteenth-century former warehouse, the shop interior is as magical as its designer clothes inspired by fairy tales. Its haute couture range has been snapped up by the likes of Madonna and Lily Allen, though you'll need a rock star's salary to afford it.

TORRES AND BRINKMANN

Rua Nova da Trindade 1b. Tues–Sat 10am–7pm, Mon 3–7pm. MAP P.53, POCKET MAP C12

Stylish, high-quality cookware including pans, coffee-making gear and griddles. There's another branch just up the road at Trav. da Trindade 18–22, specializing in porcelain, glass and silverware.

A VIDA PORTUGUESA

Rua Anchieta 11. Mon–Sat 10am–8pm. MAP P.53, POCKET MAP C12

Somewhat sparse and expensive but evocative collection of retro toys, crafts and ceramics, beautifully displayed and packaged in a historic former grocery.

Restaurants

AQUI HÁ PEIXE

Rua da Trindade 18a ☎ 213 432 154. Tues–Sun noon–3pm & 7–11pm. MAP P.53, POCKET MAP C12

Meaning "We've got fish here", this stylish seafood restaurant has been making waves even with Lisboetas who know a thing or two about the sea's produce. Classic fish dishes are served with panache – sublime tuna steaks, prawns cooked in garlic, clams cooked with coriander, plus a few meat dishes, all from around €16, in a neat fish-themed interior.

CASA LIÈGE

Rua da Bica Duarte Belo 72–74 ☎ 213 422 794. Mon–Sat 11am–11pm. MAP P.53, POCKET MAP B12

Small and bustling *tasca* at the top end of the Elevador da Bica, packed at lunchtimes thanks to filling and inexpensive dishes such as grilled chicken, sausages and fine *pastéis de bacalhau* from under €7. Good house wine, too.

CERVEJARIA FAROL

Alfredo Dinis Alex 1–3, Cacilhas ☎ 212 765 248. Daily 10am–midnight. MAP P.53, POCKET MAP H9

The most high-profile seafood restaurant in Cacilhas, with fine views across the Tejo to match. If you feel extravagant, it's hard to beat the lobsters, though other fish dishes are yours from around €9. Azulejos on the wall show the old *farol* (lighthouse) that once stood here – the restaurant is located along the quayside, on the right as you leave the ferry.

CANTINHO DO AVILLEZ

Rua dos Duques de Bragança 7 ☎ 211 992 369, ⓦ www.cantinhodoavillez.pt. Mon–Sat 12.30–3pm & 7.30pm–midnight. MAP P.53, POCKET MAP C13.

In a bright, white space, with tram #28 rattling by its door, this laidback but classy canteen is the place to sample food from Lisbon's top chef, José Avillez. Delectable mains from €14–17 include the likes of scallops with sweet potatoes, mushrooms and asparagus or tuna with ginger. Starters include a superb baked Nisa cheese and the house wines are equally top-notch.

LA BRASSERIE L'ENTRECÔTE

Rua do Alecrim 117–120 ☎ 213 473 616. Daily 12.30–3pm & 8pm–midnight. MAP P.53, POCKET MAP C12

This upmarket restaurant has won awards for its entrecôte steak which is just as well, as that's all it serves. With a sauce said to contain 35 ingredients, it is truly delicious. There's also a good set menu for around €17. Reservations advised.

CERVEJARIA FAROL

NOOBAI

Miradouro de Santa Catarina ☎ 213 465 014.
Mon–Sat noon–11pm, Sun noon–10pm. MAP
P.53, POCKET MAP A12

Modern, jazzy café-restaurant
with a superb terrace just below
Miradouro de Santa Catarina.
Fabulous views complement
the inexpensive fresh juices,
salads, quiches and the like.

PHARMACIA

Rua Marechal Saldanha 1 ☎ 213 462 146.
Tues–Sun 1pm–1am. MAP P.53, POCKET MAP A12.

Part of the Pharmaceutical
Society and Museum, this
traditional building on lawns
facing the Tejo is a terrific
spot for a quirky café-
restaurant decked out with
retro pharmacy fittings. The
speciality here is tapas (from
around €7). It also serves up
fine steaks, or just pop in for
a drink.

PORTO DE ABRIGO

Rua dos Remolares 16–18 ☎ 213 460 873.
Mon–Sat 11am–11pm. MAP P.53, POCKET MAP C13

This long-established restaurant
with a little stained-glass

window near the main market
serves good-value dishes such
as octopus, salmon and *açorda
de camarão* (shrimps with
garlicky bread sauce) from
around €8.

TAVARES

Rua da Misericórdia 35 ☎ 213 421 112.
Tues–Sat 12.30–2.30pm & 7.30–11pm.
MAP P.53, POCKET MAP C12

Lisbon's oldest restaurant,
dating from 1784, is a riot
of gilt and mirrors, a fitting
setting for Michelin-starred
cooking. This is the place to try
the best of modern Portuguese
cuisine: seafood rice, pork
and clams or *bacalhau* dishes
from €35, or a tasting menu at
around €90.

Cafés

BENARD

Rua Garrett 104. Mon–Sat 8am–midnight.
MAP P.53, POCKET MAP C12

Often overlooked because of
its proximity to *A Brasileira*,
this ornate café offers superb
cakes, ice cream and coffees;
it also has an outdoor terrace
on Chiado's most fashionable
street.

A BRASILEIRA

Rua Garrett 120. Daily 8am–2am. MAP P.53,
POCKET MAP C12

Opened in 1905, and marked
by an outdoor bronze statue
of the poet Fernando Pessoa,
this is the most famous of
Lisbon's old-style coffee houses.
The tables on the pedestrianized street get snapped up by
tourists but the real appeal is
in its traditional interior, where
prices are considerably cheaper,
especially if you stand at the
long bar. At night buskers often
add a frisson as the clientele
changes to a more youthful
brigade, all on the beer.

TAVARES

PESSOA STATUE, A BRASILEIRA

the Elevador da Bica, with occasional live jazz and Latin sounds and a moderately priced bar-food menu.

BAR BA

Praça Luis de Camões 8. Daily noon–midnight. MAP P.53, POCKET MAP C12

Swish and stylish split-level hotel bar, with a giant triangular table in the main area, a downstairs video-room and laid-back lounge area full of comfy cushions. Pricey drinks come with generous bowls of nuts. DJs man the decks from 9pm most nights of the week.

CAFÉ TATI

Rua da Ribeira Nova 36 ☎ 213 461 279. Tues–Sun 11am–1am. MAP P.53, POCKET MAP B13.

One of the new breed of arty café-bars opening in the down-at-heel area around the market. With stripped walls and old furniture, this has tatty-chic decor and a very appealing range of snacks, teas, cakes and wines. Popular for Sunday brunch, it is also lively on Wednesday and Sunday evenings when there's live jazz.

INTER MEZO

Rua Garrett Patio 19. Mon–Sat 11am–2am. MAP P.53, POCKET MAP D12

With outside seats in a hidden courtyard, this stylish little modern bar does a mean range of cocktails and other drinks; its sister *Mezo Giorno* next door also serves decent pizzas.

SOL E PESCA

Rua Nova do Carvalho 44 ☎ 213 467 203. Mon–Sat noon–11pm. MAP P.53, POCKET MAP C13.

Once a shop selling fishing equipment, this is now a hip bar on an up-and-coming street better known for its strip joints. The fishing equipment is now part of the decor, and you can still purchase tinned fish to enjoy with bread and wine.

CAFÉ VERTIGO

Travessa do Carmo 4 ☎ 213 433 112. Mon–Sat 11am–11pm, Sun 10.30am–6.30pm. MAP P.53, POCKET MAP C12

An arty crowd frequents this bare-brick walled café with an ornate glass ceiling. Occasional art exhibits and a good range of cakes and organic snacks.

LEITARIA ACADÉMICA

Largo do Carmo 1–3. Mon–Sat 7am–midnight, Sun 7am–8pm. MAP P.53, POCKET MAP C12

Outdoor tables on one of the city's leafiest squares. Besides drinks and snacks, it also does light lunches; in summer, the delicious grilled sardines are hard to beat.

Bars

BICAENSE

Rua da Bica Duarte Belo 38–42. Tues–Sat 8pm–2am. MAP P.53, POCKET MAP B12

Small, fashionable bar on the steep street used by

Bairro Alto and São Bento

The Bairro Alto, the upper town, sits on a hill west of the Baixa. After the 1755 earthquake, the relatively unscathed district became the favoured haunt of Lisbon's young bohemians. Home to the Institute of Art and Design and various designer boutiques, it is still the city's most fashionable district. By day, the central grid of narrow, cobbled streets feels residential. After dark, however, the area throngs with people visiting its famed fado houses, bars and restaurants, while the city's gay community coalesces around the clubs of clubs of neighbouring Princípe Real. There are impressive monuments too including the Palácio da Assembléia, Portugal's parliamentary building in nearby São Bento. This area houses good ethnic restaurants, a legacy of the city's first black community established by the descendents of African slaves.

ELEVADOR DA GLÓRIA

Mon–Fri 7am–midnight, Sat 8.30am–2am, Sun 9am–midnight. €3.50 return. MAP P.62–63, POCKET MAP C11

Everyone should ride the Elevador da Glória at least once. From the bottom of Calçada da Glória (off Praça dos Restauradores, see p.33), the funicular climbs the knee-jarringly sheer street in a couple of minutes, leaving the lower city behind as you ascend above its rooftops. An amazing feat of engineering, the tram system was built in 1885. It was originally powered by water displacement before this was replaced by steam before electricity was introduced.

At the top, pause at the gardens, the **Miradouro de São Pedro de Alcântara**, from where there's a superb view across the city to the castle.

ELEVADOR DA GLÓRIA

IGREJA DE SÃO ROQUE

Largo de Trindade Coelha ☎ 213 235 065, Ⓦwww.museu-saoroque.com. Mon 2–6pm, Tues–Wed & Fri–Sun 9am–6pm, Thurs 9am–9pm. Free. MAP P.62–63, POCKET MAP C11

The sixteenth-century Igreja de São Roque looks like the plainest church in the city, with its bleak Renaissance facade. Yet inside lies an astonishing succession of lavishly decorated side chapels. The highlight is the **Capela de São João Baptista**, for its size the most expensive chapel ever constructed. It was ordered from Rome in 1742 by Dom João V to honour his patron saint and, more dubiously, to gratify Pope Benedict XIV whom he had persuaded to confer a patriarchate on Lisbon. It was erected at the Vatican for the Pope to celebrate Mass in, before being dismantled and shipped to Lisbon at the then vast cost of £250,000. If you examine the four "oil paintings" of John the Baptist's life, you'll find that they are in fact intricately worked mosaics. The more valuable parts of the altar front are kept in the adjacent **museum** (Tues–Wed & Fri–Sun 10am–6pm, Thurs 2–9pm. €2.50, free Sun 10am–2pm), which also displays sixteenth- to eighteenth-century paintings and a motley collection of church relics.

CONVENTO DO CARMO

Entrance on Largo do Carmo ☎ 213 478 629. Mon–Sat: June–Sept 10am–7pm; Oct–May 10am–6pm. €4. MAP P.53, POCKET MAP D12

Built between 1389 and 1423, and once the largest church in the city, the Convento do Carmo was partially destroyed by the 1755 earthquake but is even more striking as a result with its beautiful Gothic arches rising grandly into the sky. Today it houses the splendid

CONVENTO DO CARMO

Museu Arqueológico do Carmo, home to many of the treasures from monasteries that were dissolved after the 1834 revolution. The entire nave is open to the elements, with columns and statuary scattered in all corners. Inside, on either side of what was the main altar, are the main exhibits, centring on a series of tombs. Largest is the beautifully carved, stone tomb of Ferdinand I; nearby, that of Gonçalo de Sousa, chancellor to Henry the Navigator, is topped by a statue of Gonçalo himself. There is also an Egyptian sarcophagus, whose inhabitant's feet are just visible underneath the lid; and, equally alarmingly, two pre-Columbian mummies which lie in glass cases, alongside the preserved heads of a couple of Peruvian Indians.

The exit to the **Elevador de Santa Justa** (see p.32) is at the side of the Convento do Carmo – go onto the rampway leading to it for fine views over the city.

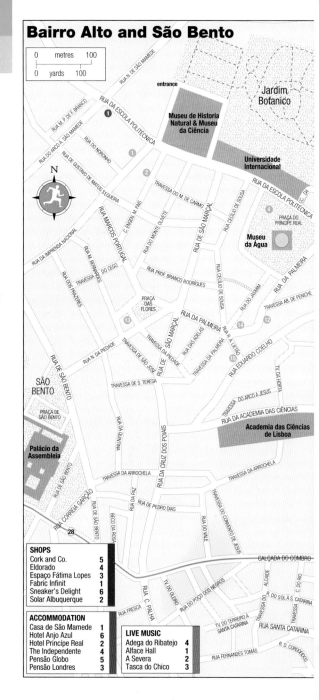

Bairro Alto and São Bento

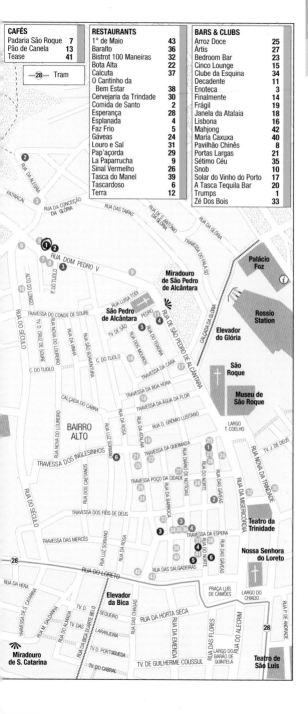

CAFÉS	
Padaria São Roque	7
Pão de Canela	13
Tease	41

—28— Tram

RESTAURANTS	
1° de Maio	43
Baralto	36
Bistrot 100 Maneiras	32
Bota Alta	22
Calcuta	37
O Cantinho da Bem Estar	38
Cervejaria da Trindade	30
Comida de Santo	2
Esperança	28
Esplanada	4
Faz Frio	5
Gáveas	24
Louro e Sal	31
Pap'açorda	29
La Paparrucha	9
Sinal Vermelho	26
Tasca do Manel	39
Tascardoso	6
Terra	12

BARS & CLUBS	
Arroz Doce	25
Ártis	27
Bedroom Bar	23
Cinco Lounge	15
Clube da Esquina	34
Decadente	11
Enoteca	3
Finalmente	14
Frágil	19
Janela da Atalaia	18
Lisbona	16
Mahjong	42
Maria Caxuxa	40
Pavilhão Chinês	8
Portas Largas	21
Sétimo Céu	35
Snob	10
Solar do Vinho do Porto	17
A Tasca Tequila Bar	20
Trumps	1
Zé Dos Bois	33

Map labels:

PATRIARCAL
RUA DA ALEGRIA
RUA DA CONCEIÇÃO DA GLÓRIA
RUA DAS TAIPAS
RUA DE S. ANTONIO DA GLÓRIA
RUA DA GLÓRIA
TRAVESSA DO FORNO
RUA DOM PEDRO V
ALTO DO LONGO
P. DO TIJOLO
Palácio Foz
Miradouro de São Pedro de Alcântara
São Pedro de Alcântara
Rua Luisa Todi
TRAVESSA DO CONDE DE SOURE
RUA NOVA DO LOUREIRO
RUA D. CRUZ DE SOURE
RUA DA VINHA
RUA SÃO BUENAVENTURA
TV. DE SÃO
PEDRO
RUA DOS MOUROS
RUA DO TEIXEIRA
RUA DE SÃO PEDRO DE ALCÂNTARA
CALÇADA DA GLÓRIA
Rossio Station
Elevador do Glória
ALTO DO SÉCULO
C. DO TIJOLO
C. DO TIJOLO
São Roque
TRAVESSA DA CARA
Museu de São Roque
CALÇADA DO CABRA
RUA DA ROSA
RUA DA ATALAIA
TRAVESSA DA BOA HORA
TRAVESSA DA ÁGUA DE FLOR
RUA D. GRÉMIO LUSITANO
LARGO T. COELHO
BAIRRO ALTO
RUA NOVA DO LOUREIRO
RUA LUZ SORIANO
TRAVESSA DOS INGLESINHOS
TRAVESSA DA QUEIMADA
RUA DIÁRIO DE NOTÍCIAS
RUA DO NORTE
RUA DAS GÁVEAS
RUA NOVA DA TRINDADE
TV. J. DE DEUS
TRAVESSA POÇO DA CIDADE
RUA DA BARROCA
RUA DOS CAETANOS
RUA DO SÉCULO
TRAVESSA DOS FIÉIS DE DEUS
RUA DA MISERICÓRDIA
Teatro da Trindade
TRAVESSA DAS MERCÊS
RUA LUZ SORIANO
RUA DA ROSA
TRAVESSA DA ESPERA
RUA DO NORTE
RUA DAS GÁVEAS
Nossa Senhora do Loreto
28
RUA DO LORETO
RUA DAS SALGADEIRAS
PRAÇA LUÍS DE CAMÕES
LARGO DO CHIADO
RUA DA HERA
Elevador da Bica
TV. D. SEQUEIRO
RUA DA HORTA SECA
RUA DAS FLORES
RUA DO ALECRIM
RUA P. DE ANDRADE
TRAVESSA DE S. CABRINA
RUA M. SALDANHA
TV. DAS CHAGAS
RUA DO ALAMEDA
RUA DA BICA DUARTE BELO
LARANJEIRA
TV. D. PORTUGUESA
RUA DA EMENDA
LARGO DO BARÃO DE QUINTELA
28
Miradouro de S. Catarina
TV. DO CABRAL
TV. DE GUILHERME COUSSUL
Teatro de São Luís

BAIRRO ALTO

MAP P.62-63, POCKET MAP B11

Quiet by day, the graffitied central streets of the Bairro Alto buzz with people after dark, especially on summer weekends when the streets become a giant mass of partygoers. The most lively area is the tight network of streets to the west of Rua da Misericórdia, particularly after midnight in Rua do Norte, Rua Diário de Notícias, Rua da Atalaia and Rua da Rosa. Running steeply downhill, Rua do Século is one of the area's most historic streets. A sign at no. 89 marks the birthplace of the Marquês de Pombal, the minister responsible for rebuilding Lisbon after the Great Earthquake.

PRAÇA DO PRÍNCIPE REAL

Bus #758 or 778 from Chiado. MAP P.62-63, POCKET MAP A10

North of the Bairro Alto, the streets open out around the leafy Praça do Príncipe Real, one of the city's loveliest squares. Laid out in 1860 and surrounded by the ornate homes of former aristocrats – now mostly offices – the square is the focal point of Lisbon's gay scene, though by day it is largely populated by families

in the local play park or locals playing cards under the trees.

MUSEU DA ÁGUA PRÍNCIPE REAL

Praça do Príncipe Real ☎ 218 100 215. Mon-Sat 10am–6pm. €1.50. Tours Wed & Sat 11am & 3pm & Fri 1pm, €2.50. Bus #758 or 778 from Chiado. MAP P.62-63, POCKET MAP A10

The Museu da Água Príncipe Real is accessed down steps in the centre of the square of the same name. Inside is an eerie nineteenth-century reservoir, where you can admire brick and vaulted ceilings, part of a network of tunnels that link up with the Aqueduto das Águas Livres (see p.98). Tours – not for claustrophobics – take you along one of these, a humid 410m tunnel that exits at the viewpoint of Miradouro de São Pedro (see p.60).

MUSEUS DE POLITÉCNICA

Rua Escola Politécnica 56 ⓦ www.mnhnc.ul.pt. Tues–Fri 10am–5pm, Sat & Sun 11am–6pm; closed Aug. €4 per museum, combined ticket €10, includes entry to temporary exhibitions and Jardim Botânico. Bus #758 or 778 from Chiado. MAP P.62-63, POCKET MAP H5

The nineteenth-century Neoclassical former technical college now hosts the mildly engaging museums of science and natural history known as the Museus de Politécnica. The **Museu da Ciência** has some absorbing geological exhibits and a low-tech interactive section where you can balance balls on jets of air and swing pendulums among throngs of school kids.

The **Museu da Historia Natural** opposite, houses a rather dreary collection of stuffed animals, eggs and shells, though temporary exhibitions can be more diverting.

JARDIM BOTÂNICO

Rua Escola Politécnica 58 ☎ 213 921 800, ⓦwww.jb.ul.pt. April–Oct Mon–Fri 9am–8pm, Sat & Sun 10am–6pm; Nov–March Mon–Fri 9am–6pm, Sat & Sun 10am–6pm. €1.50 gardens, €2.50 includes "Lugartagis", or €10 for combined ticket to Museus de Politécnica. MAP P.62-63, POCKET MAP H5

The lush botanical gardens are almost invisible from the surrounding streets and provide a tranquil escape from the city bustle. The Portuguese explorers introduced many plant species to Europe during the golden age of exploration and these gardens, laid out between 1858 and 1878, are packed with twenty thousand neatly labelled species from around the world. Shady paths lead downhill under towering palms and luxuriant shrubs past a "Lugartagis" greenhouse for breeding butterflies.

PALÁCIO DA ASSEMBLÉIA

Tram #28. MAP P.62-63, POCKET MAP H6

Below the Bairro Alto in the district of São Bento, you can't miss the late sixteenth-century Neoclassical facade of the Palácio da Assembléia. Formerly a Benedictine monastery, it was taken over by the government in 1834 and today houses the *Assembléia da República*, Portugal's **parliament**; it's not open to the public, though you can arrange a tour by special arrangement (☎ 213 919 000, ⓦwww.parlamento.pt). Most visitors make do with the view of its steep white steps from tram #28 as it rattles along Calçada da Estrela, though it is worth exploring the surprisingly earthy streets nearby. This was where Lisbon's black community put down roots – Rua do Poço dos Negros (black man's well) takes its awful name from the corpses of slaves tossed into a hole here.

CASA MUSEU AMÁLIA RODRIGUES

Rua de São Bento 193 ☎ 213 971 896, ⓦwww.amaliarodrigues.pt. Tues–Sun 10am–1pm & 2–6pm. €5. Bus #706 from Praça do Comércio, or a short walk from tram #28. MAP P.62-63, POCKET MAP G6

The daughter of an Alfama orange-seller, Amália Rodrigues was the undisputed queen of fado music until her death in 1999. The house where she lived since the 1950s has been kept as it was, and you can also admire original posters advertising her performances on stage and in the cinema, portraits by Portuguese artists and some of her personal possessions.

JARDIM BOTÂNICO

Shops

CORK AND CO.

Rua das Salgadeiras 10. Mon–Wed
noon–10pm, Thurs–Sat noon–midnight.
MAP P.63, POCKET MAP B12.
Portugal supplies around fifty
percent of the world's cork, and
this stylish shop displays the
versatility of the product with
a range of tasteful cork goods,
from bags and bracelets to
umbrellas.

ELDORADO

Rua do Norte 23–25. Mon–Sat 2pm–
midnight. MAP P.62-63, POCKET MAP C12
An interesting mixture of
clubbing gear and secondhand
castoffs alongside old records
and CDs, aimed at Lisbon's
young groovers. A good place
to head for if you need a new
wardrobe for a night out
without breaking the bank.

ESPAÇO FÁTIMA LOPES

Rua da Atalaia 36. Mon–Fri 10am–1.30pm
& 2.30–8pm, Sat 11.30am–2.30pm &
3.30–8.30pm. MAP P.62-63, POCKET MAP B12
One of the few large shops in
the Bairro Alto and flagship
store for the confident designs
of Portugal's top designer,
Fátima Lopes. Born in Madeira,
Lopes has carved out a niche
with elegant, youthful clothes
and has branched out into
classy jewellery and homeware
There's also a bar, though it's
only open sporadically.

FABRIC INFINIT

Rua Dom Pedro V 74. Tues–Sat 11am–7pm.
MAP P.62-63, POCKET MAP B10
Upmarket store selling
one-off and unique designer
jewellery, shoes and home
products; should you tire of
browsing there's an attractive
café, selling organic produce,
complete with Zen garden
patio at the back.

SNEAKER'S DELIGHT

SNEAKER'S DELIGHT

Rua do Norte 30–32. Mon–Sat 1–10pm.
MAP P.62-63, POCKET MAP C12
A typical example of Bairro
Alto creativity – limited edition
sneakers and a few designer
clothes in a sparse space dotted
with bits of old TVs and
computers that are a work of art
in their own right.

SOLAR ALBUQUERQUE

Rua Dom Pedro V 68–70. Daily 10am–7pm,
closed weekends in July and Aug. MAP P.62-63,
POCKET MAP B10
A huge treasure-trove of
antique tiles, plates and
ceramics dating back to the
sixteenth century – great for a
browse.

Restaurants

1º DE MAIO

Rua da Atalaia 8 ☎ 213 426 840. Daily
noon–3pm & 7–11pm, Sat 7–11pm.
MAP P.62-63, POCKET MAP B12
Naked Chef-style food: simple
slabs of grilled fish and meat
with boiled veg and chips. You
can watch the cook through a
hatch at the back, adding to the

theatrics of a bustling, traditional *adega* (wine cellar) with a low, arched ceiling. Mains are around €10. Get there early to be sure of a table.

BARALTO

Rua do Diário de Notícias 31 ☎ 213 426 739. Mon–Sat 7pm–midnight. MAP P.62–63. POCKET MAP B12

A cosy tiled place with efficient service – along with the usual fish and meat you'll find unusual dishes such as tuna pie and duck rice from around €12.

BISTROT 100 MANEIRAS

Largo da Trindade 9 ☎ 210 990 475. Mon–Sat 11am–11pm. MAP P.63, POCKET MAP C12.

In a fine Art Nouveau building, this is the latest offering from Sarajevo-born chef Ljubmar Stanisic, whose restaurant and canteen serve a fascinating mixture of classy mains (suckling pig, fresh fish, around €25) and upmarket comfort foods such as salmon sausages and deluxe hamburgers (€17).

BOTA ALTA

Trav. da Queimada 37 ☎ 213 427 959. Mon–Fri noon–2.30pm & 7–10.30pm, Sat 7–10pm. MAP P.62–63. POCKET MAP B11

Tavern decorated with old b°oots (*botas*) and an eclectic picture collection. It attracts queues for its vast portions of sensibly priced traditional Portuguese food – including *bacalhau com natas* (cod cooked in cream) and fine cakes. The tables are crammed in and it's always packed; try to arrive before 8pm or book in advance. Mains from €10.

CALCUTA

Rua do Norte 17 ☎ 213 428 295. Mon–Sat noon–midnight, Sun 6pm–midnight. MAP P.62–63, POCKET MAP C12

Very popular Indian restaurant attracting a youngish clientele. Lots of chicken, seafood and lamb curries, tandoori dishes, and good vegetarian options with mains from around €9. Reservations are advised.

O CANTINHO DO BEM ESTAR

Rua do Norte 46. ☎ 213 464 265. Tues–Sun 7–11pm. MAP P.62–63, POCKET MAP C12

Small and popular, the "canteen of well-being" lives up to its name: get there early to guarantee a place. From the menu, the rice dishes and generous salads are the best bet.

CERVEJARIA DA TRINDADE

Rua Nova da Trindade 20 ☎ 213 423 506. Daily 10am–midnight. MAP P.62–63, POCKET MAP C11

The city's oldest beer-hall dates from 1836. At busy times you'll be shown to your table; at others, avoid the dull modern extensions and find a space in the original vaulted hall, decorated with azulejos, depicting the elements and seasons. Shellfish is the speciality, though other fish and meat dishes (from €10) are lighter on the wallet. There is also a patio garden and – a rarity – a children's menu.

BOTA ALTA

COMIDA DE SANTO

Calçada Engenheiro Miguel Pais 39 ☎ 213 963 339. Daily 12.30–3.30pm & 7.30pm–1am. Closed June–Sept. MAP P.62–63, POCKET MAP H6

Late-opening, slightly pricey Brazilian restaurant serving cocktails and classic dishes such as *feijoada a brasileira* (Brazilian bean stew) and a fantastic *ensopadinho de peixe* (fish in coconut), with vegetarian options. Mains around €15–18.

ESPERANÇA

Rua do Norte 95 ☎ 213 432 027. Tues–Fri 8pm–2am, Sat & Sun 1pm–4pm & 8pm–2am. MAP P.62–63, POCKET MAP C11

Fashionable and jazzy haunt for mid-priced Italian dishes including filling pasta dishes, fine risottos and decent pizzas, all from around €9.

ESPLANADA

Praça do Príncipe Real ☎ 962 311 669. Daily 9am–11pm. MAP P.62–63, POCKET MAP A10

A good range of quiches and chunky sandwiches makes this an ideal and inexpensive lunch spot. The outdoor tables set under the trees get snapped up quickly, though the glass

pavilion comes into its own when the weather turns. It's also a popular gay haunt.

FAZ FRIO

Rua Dom Pedro V 96–98 ☎ 213 461 860. Daily noon–midnight; usually closed late Aug–late Sept. MAP P.62–63, POCKET MAP B10

A traditional restaurant, replete with coloured tiles and confessional-like cubicles. The huge portions of *bacalhau*, seafood paella and prawns in breadcrumbs are good value, as are a variety of dishes of the day. Mains €9–10.

GÁVEAS

Rua das Gáveas 82–84 ☎ 213 426 460. Mon–Fri noon–3pm & 7.30–11.30pm, Sat 7.30–11.30pm. MAP P.62–63, POCKET MAP C11

Good-value if spartan *adega* (wine cellar) with reliable dishes of the day and a long menu featuring pasta, *açorda*, meats and *bacalhau*. Mains around €9–10.

LOURO E SAL

Rua da Atalaia 53 ☎ 213 476 275. Daily except Tuesday 7pm–12.30am. MAP P.62–63, POCKET MAP B12

Typical of a new breed of fashionable restaurants in the area, offering good-value nouveau Portuguese cuisine such as tuna in pastry and salmon with capers, with mains from around €10.

PAP'AÇORDA

Rua da Atalaia 57–59 ☎ 213 464 811. Tues–Sat 12.30–2pm & 8–11.30pm. MAP P.62–63, POCKET MAP B11

Renowned restaurant that attracts Lisbon's fashionable elite to its chandelier-hung dining room. *Açorda* is the house speciality There are also regional dishes (including mixed fish with aleoli) and fine starters such as oysters or tiger prawns. Mains start at €17. Reservations are advised.

LA PAPARRUCHA

Rua Dom Pedro V 18–20 ☎ 213 425 333.
Mon–Fri noon–3pm & 7pm–2am, Sat & Sun
noon–4pm & 7pm–2am. MAP P.62-63, POCKET
MAP B10

The best feature of this Argentinian restaurant is the fantastic back room and terrace offering superb views over the Baixa. The food is recommended too, especially if you like steaks, though the fish, pasta and vegetarian options are also great. Mains from €14, with good-value lunchtime buffets from around €10.

SINAL VERMELHO

Rua das Gáveas 89 ☎ 213 461 252. Mon–Sat
12.30–2.30pm & 7.30–11.30pm; closed July.
MAP P.62-63, POCKET MAP C11

Roomy *adega* (wine cellar) that's popular with Lisbon's moneyed youth. Specialities (€10–14) include well-presented *açorda de gambas* (prawns in garlicky bread sauce) and *arroz de polvo* (octopus rice), and there's an impressive wine list. It is best to book ahead.

TASCA DO MANEL

Rua da Barroca 24 ☎ 213 463 813. Mon–Sat
noon–3pm & 7.30–11pm. MAP P.62-63, POCKET
MAP C12

One of the dying breed of inexpensive *tascas* in this district, still attracting a largely local crowd for wholesome dishes such as wild boar, grilled salmon or squid from around €10.

TASCARDOSO

Rua Dom Pedro V 137 ☎ 213 427 578. Mon–
Sat noon–3pm & 7pm–midnight. MAP P.62-63,
POCKET MAP A10

Go through the stand-up bar and down the stairs to the tiny eating area for excellent and inexpensive tapas-style meats and cheeses and good-value hot dishes from around €7.

TERRA

TERRA

Rua da Palmeira 15 ☎ 707 108 108. Tues–
Sun 12.30–3.30pm & 7.30–midnight. MAP
P.62-63, POCKET MAP A10

Attractive vegetarian and vegan restaurant with a lovely patio garden and well-priced salads and pasta dishes. The all-you-can-eat buffets are good value at around €16; leave room for the Italian ice creams.

Cafés

PADARIA SÃO ROQUE

Rua Dom Pedro V 57c. Daily 7am–7pm. MAP
P.62-63, POCKET MAP B10

Also known as *Catedral do Pão*, this is a corner café-bakery with a wonderfully ornate high ceiling. You can have coffee and croissants at the counter or buy fresh pastries to take away.

PÃO DE CANELA

Praça das Flôres 27–28. Tues–Sun
7.30am–11pm, Mon 7.30am–8pm. MAP P.62-63,
POCKET MAP H6

Pretty, tile-fronted café serving great pastries, soups and snacks. The outdoor terrace faces a children's play area on this lovely square.

CLUBE DA ESQUINA

TEASE

Rua do Norte 31–33. Mon–Thurs 1–9pm,
Fri–Sat noon–11pm, Sun 2–8pm. MAP P.62-63,
POCKET MAP C12

Unusual for this part of town,
this café-cum-bar has soft
velvet sofas to slump in while
you sip herbal teas, infusions or
delicious cupcakes – or if you
fancy something stronger, a
fruit cocktail.

Bars and clubs

ARROZ DOCE

Rua da Atalaia 117–119 ☎ 213 462 601.
Mon–Sat noon–3am. MAP P.62-63, POCKET
MAP B11

An unpretentious bar in the
middle of the frenetic Bairro
Alto, with friendly owners;
try "Auntie's" sangria and the
evening will never be the same.

ÁRTIS

Rua do Diário de Notícias 95 ☎ 213 424 795.
Tues–Fri 6pm–2am, Sat & Sun 6pm–3am. MAP
P.62-63, POCKET MAP B11

A fashionable tapas bar – a
good place to sample local
wines while tapas (€4–6)
includes tasty pork with

coriander and garlic, local
cheeses and spicy chouriço.

BEDROOM BAR

Rua do Norte 86 ☎ 213 431 631. Mon–Sat
10pm–3am. MAP P.62-63, POCKET MAP C11

This large, flash space has
taken the lounge bar concept a
step further by installing beds
where you can chill out with a
cocktail – though the pulsing
music keeps most of the action
away from the sheets.

CINCO LOUNGE

Rua Ruben A. Leitão 179. Daily 9pm–2am.
MAP P.62-63, POCKET MAP A11

A New York-style cocktail
lounge run by Brits in the heart
of Lisbon – there are over a
hundred cocktails to choose
from; go for one of the wacky
fruit concoctions (anyone
for hazelnut and vanilla?)
while sinking into one of the
enormous comfy sofas.

CLUBE DA ESQUINA

Rua da Barroca 30 ☎ 213 427 149. Daily
9.30pm–2am. MAP P.62-63, POCKET MAP B12

Buzzing little corner bar with
ancient radios on the walls and
DJs spinning discs. Attracts
a young crowd enjoying vast
measures of spirits.

DECADENTE BAR

Rua de São Pedro de Alcântara 81 ☎ 213 461
281. Daily 6pm–2am. MAP P.63, POCKET MAP B11.

Attached to a boutique hostel,
this small, fashionable bar
attracts a youthful, laidback
crowd. It's best on Thursday
and Saturday evening when
there is often live music,
usually Latin or jazz.

ENOTECA

Rua da Mãe de Agua ☎ 213 422 079. Tues–
Sun 6pm–2am. MAP P.62-63, POCKET MAP B10

This extraordinary wine
bar is set in the bowels of a
nineteenth-century bathhouse

whose underground tunnels once piped water into Lisbon. The bar offers a long list of Portuguese wines, which you can enjoy with regional breads and assorted *petiscos* (snacks) such as oysters or dates with bacon. It gets busy at weekends so it's best to reserve if you want to eat, though you can always squeeze in for a drink or sit at one of the outside tables.

FINALMENTE

Rua da Palmeira 38 ☎ 213 479 923. Daily 11am–6am. MAP P.62-63, POCKET MAP A10

A gay disco with lashings of kitsch, famed for its drag shows (at 2am) featuring skimpily dressed "*senhoritas*" camping it up to high-tech sounds.

FRÁGIL

Rua da Atalaia 126 ☎ 213 469 578, Ⓦ www .fragil.com.pt. Mon-Sat 11.30pm–4am. MAP P.62-63, POCKET MAP B11

This has long been one of Lisbon's most popular clubs, and it remains very lively, particularly from Thursday to Saturday, though it doesn't really get going until after 1am. It's wonderfully pretentious and has a strict door policy (it helps if you're young and beautiful). You'll need to ring the bell to get in.

JANELA DA ATALAIA

Rua da Atalaia 160 ☎ 213 465 988. Mon-Thurs 10pm–2am, Fri-Sat 9.30pm–3am. MAP P.62-63, POCKET MAP B11

A fine old bar with two rooms, inexpensive drinks and laid-back sounds, usually world music. Most Wednesdays there's a band, often salsa/ Brazilian.

LISBONA

Rua da Atalaia 196 ☎ 213 471 412. Mon-Sat 6pm–2am. MAP P.62-63 POCKET MAP B11

Earthy bar attracting its fair share of local characters and Bairro Alto trendies. Decor is basic – chequerboard tiles covered in soccer memorabilia, old film posters and graffiti – but there's catchy pop music and good beer.

MAHJONG

Rua da Atalaia 3 ☎ 213 421 039. Daily 7pm–2am. MAP P.62-63, POCKET MAP B12

At the bottom of the Bairro Alto and traditionally a place to start an evening before moving on up. It's a great space, with plain white tiles and a rough wooden bar juxtaposed with modern Chinese motifs – the clientele are similarly eclectic.

MARIA CAXUXA

Rua da Barroca 6–12 ☎ 965 039 094. Daily 5pm–2am. MAP P.63, POCKET MAP B12.

This arty lounge bar has plenty of space for big sofas and eclectic decor – including record players and aged machinery – though these get lost in the crowds when the DJ pumps up the volume as the evening progresses.

BAIRRO ALTO

PAVILHÃO CHINÊS

Rua Dom Pedro V 89 ☎ 213 424 729. Mon–Sat 6pm–2am, Sun 9pm–2am. MAP P.62–63, POCKET MAP B10

Once a nineteenth-century tea and coffee merchants' shop, this is now a quirky bar set in a series of comfy rooms, including a pool room. Most are lined with mirrored cabinets containing a bizarre range of 4,000 artefacts from around the world, including a cabinet of model trams. There's waiter service and the usual drinks are supplemented by a long list of exotic cocktails.

PORTAS LARGAS

Rua da Atalaia 105 ☎ 218 466 379. Daily 6pm–2am. MAP P.62–63, POCKET MAP B11

The bar's *portas largas* (big doors) are usually thrown wide open, inviting the neighbourhood into this friendly black-and-white-tiled *adega* (wine cellar). There are cheapish drinks, music from fado to pop, and a young, mixed gay and straight clientele, which spills onto the streets before hitting *Frágil*, just over the road.

SÉTIMO CÉU

Trav. da Espera 54 ☎ 213 466 471. Mon–Sat 10pm–2am. MAP P.62–63, POCKET MAP B12

An obligatory stop for gays and lesbians, who imbibe beers and *caipirinhas* served by the Brazilian owner. The great atmosphere spills out onto the street.

SOLAR DO VINHO DO PORTO

Rua de São Pedro de Alcântara 45 ☎ 213 475 707, ⓦ www.ivp.pt. Mon–Fri 11am–midnight, Sat 2pm–midnight. MAP P.62–63, POCKET MAP B11

The eighteenth-century Palácio Ludovice is home to the Lisbon branch of the Port Wine Institute, responsible for promoting one of Portugal's most famous exports. Visitors are lured in with over three hundred types of port, starting at around €2 a glass and rising to some €25 for a glass of forty-year-old J.W. Burmester. Drinks (as well as hams and cheeses) are served at low tables in the mansion's stylishly designed interior. The waiters are notoriously snooty but it's still a good place to kick off an evening.

SOLAR DO VINHO DO PORTO

SNOB

Rua do Século 178 ☎ 213 463 723. Daily
4.30pm–3am. MAP P.62-63, POCKET MAP A10

Cosy and upmarket bar and
restaurant, full of media types
enjoying cocktails. It's a good
late-night option which also
serves inexpensive steaks or
light snacks.

A TASCA TEQUILA BAR

Trav. da Queimada 13–15. Daily 6pm–3am.
MAP P.62-63, POCKET MAP C11

Colourful Mexican bar with
Latin sounds, which caters to
a good-time crowd downing
tequilas, margaritas and
Brazilian *caipirinhas*.

ZÉ DOS BOIS

Rua da Barroca 59 ☎ 213 430 205, Ⓦ www
.zedebois.org. Wed–Sun 11pm–2am. MAP
P.62-63, POCKET MAP B12

Rambling arts venue in an
eighteenth-century palace that
hosts installations, films and
exhibitions (hours vary – phone
for details) along with occasional
concerts. At weekends, local
DJs showcase their talents to a
bohemian crowd.

Live music

ALFACE HALL

Rua do Norte 96 ☎ 213 433 293. Daily
5pm–2am. MAP P.63, POCKET MAP C11

This quirky café-bar is in a
former print works. Now part
of a hostel and filled with retro
chairs and artefacts, its high
ceilings and comfy sofas make
it an ideal place to hang out
for live music, usually jazz, on
Wed–Sun from 10pm.

ADEGA DO RIBATEJO

Rua do Diário de Notícias 23 ☎ 213 468
343. Mon–Sat noon–midnight. MAP P.62-63,
POCKET MAP B12

This great fado club has been
a favoured haunt for British

PORTUGUESE GUITAR

artists Gilbert and George.
It is touristy but fun. The
singers include a couple of
professionals, the manager
and – best of all – the cooks.
Also has one of the lowest
minimum charges (around
€15) although the accompa-
nying food is both expensive
and indifferent.

A SEVERA

Rua das Gáveas 51–61 ☎ 213 428 314,
Ⓦ www.asevera.com. Mon–Tues & Thurs–Sun
8pm–3am. MAP P.62-63, POCKET MAP C12

A city institution, named
after the nineteenth-century
singer Maria Severa. The club
attracts big fado names and
equally large prices. Minimum
consumption of €20 builds
to more like €40 with food
(served until midnight).

TASCA DO CHICO

Rua do Diário de Notícias 39 ☎ 213 431 040.
Daily 7pm–2am. MAP P.62-63, POCKET MAP B12

Atmospheric little bar (a fine
spot for a drink) which morphs
into a very popular fado bar
on Mon & Wed, when crowds
pack in to hear moving fado
from 8pm.

Estrela, Lapa and Santos

West of the Bairro Alto sits the leafy district of Estrela, best known for its gardens and enormous basilica. To the south lies opulent Lapa, Lisbon's diplomatic quarter, sheltering some of its top hotels. Sumptuous mansions and grand embassy buildings peer out majestically towards the Tejo. The superb Museu Nacional de Arte Antiga below here is Portugal's national gallery, while down on the riverfront, Santos is promoted as "the district of design" with some of the city's coolest shops and bars along with some long-established clubs.

BASÍLICA AND JARDIM DA ESTRELA

Basílica daily 7.30am–1pm & 3–8pm. Free. Tram #28 or 25. MAP OPPOSITE, POCKET MAP G6

The impressive Basílica da Estrela is a vast monument to late eighteenth-century Neoclassicism. Constructed by order of Queen Maria I (whose tomb lies within), and completed in 1790, its landmark white dome can be seen from much of the city. Opposite is the **Jardim da Estrela** (daily, free), one of the city's most enjoyable gardens; it is a quiet refuge with a pond-side café, a well-equipped children's playground and even a library kiosk for those who fancy sampling Portuguese literature under the palms.

CEMITÉRIO DOS INGLESES

Rua São Jorge 6 ☎ 213 906 248. Mon–Fri 10am–1pm. Tram #28 or 25. MAP OPPOSITE, POCKET MAP G6

The name translates as "The English Cemetery" but it is actually a cemetery for all Protestants, founded in 1717. Here, among the cypresses and tombs of various expatriates, lie the remains of Henry Fielding. He came to Lisbon hoping the climate would improve his failing health, but his inability to recuperate may have influenced his verdict on Lisbon as "the nastiest city in the world".

BASÍLICA DA ESTRELA

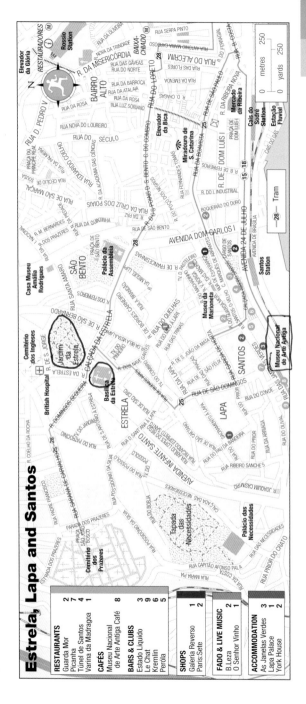

Estrela, Lapa and Santos

RESTAURANTS

Guarda Mor	2
Picanha	7
Tunel de Santos	4
Varina da Madragoa	1

CAFÉS

Museu Nacional de Arte Antiga Café	8

BARS & CLUBS

Estado Liquido	3
Le Chat	9
Kremlin	6
Pérola	5

SHOPS

Galeria Reverso	1
Paris·Sete	2

FADO & LIVE MUSIC

B.Leza	2
O Senhor Vinho	1

ACCOMMODATION

As Janelas Verdes	3
Lapa Palace	1
York House	2

LAPA

MAP P.75, POCKET MAP F7

From Estrela tram 25# skirts past the well-heeled district of Lapa on its way down to the waterfront. Lapa is the most desired address in the city and though it contains no sights as such, it is worth wandering around to admire the stunning mansions. A good route is to follow the tram tracks from Estrela and turn right into Rua do Sacramento à Lapa, past fantastic embassy buildings. Turn left into Rua do Pau da Bandeira past the plush *Lapa Palace* hotel (if you have the funds, you can have a drink at the bar). From here, go left into Rua do Prior and right into Rua do Conde and it's a ten-minute walk downhill to the Museu Nacional de Arte Antiga (see below).

MUSEU NACIONAL DE ARTE ANTIGA

Rua das Janelas Verdes 95 ☎213 912 800, ☉www.mnarteantiga-ipmuseus.pt. Tues 2–6pm, Wed–Sun 10am–6pm. €5, free Sun 10am–2pm. Bus #760, #713 or #727 or a short walk from tram #25. MAP P.75, POCKET MAP G8

The Museu Nacional de Arte Antiga features the largest collection of Portuguese fifteenth- and sixteenth-century paintings in the country, European art from the fourteenth century to the present day and a rich display of applied art. All of this is well exhibited in a tastefully converted seventeenth-century palace once owned by the Marquês de Pombal. The museum uses ten "reference points" to guide you round the collection. The prinicipal highlight is **Nuno Gonçalves's altarpiece** dedicated to St Vincent (1467–70), a brilliantly marshalled composition depicting Lisbon's patron saint receiving homage from all ranks of its citizens, their faces appearing remarkably modern. The other main highlight is Hieronymus Bosch's stunningly gruesome *Temptation of St Anthony* in room 57 (don't miss the image on the back of the painting, showing the arrest of Christ). Elsewhere, seek out the altar panel depicting the *Resurrection* by Raphael; Francisco de Zurbarán's *The Twelve Apostles;* a small statue of a nymph by Auguste Rodin and works by Albrecht Dürer, Holbein, Cranach (particularly

Salome), Fragonard and Josefa de Óbidos, considered one of Portugal's greatest female painters.

The **Oriental art** collection shows how the Portuguese were influenced by overseas designs encountered during the sixteenth century. There is inlaid furniture from Goa, Turkish and Syrian azulejos, Qing Dynasty porcelain and a fantastic series of late sixteenth-century Japanese *namban* screens (room 14), depicting the Portuguese landing at Nagasaki. The Japanese regarded the Portuguese traders as southern barbarians (*namban*) with large noses – hence their Pinocchio-like features. The museum extends over the remains of the sixteenth-century St Albert monastery, most of which was razed during the 1755 earthquake, although its beautiful chapel can still be seen today, downstairs by the main entrance. Don't miss the garden café, either (see p.78).

MUSEU DA MARIONETA

Rua da Esperança 146 ☎ 213 942 810. Tues–Sun 10am–1pm & 2–5.30pm. €5, children €3, free Sun 10am–1pm. Tram #25 then a short walk. MAP P.75, POCKET MAP G7

Contemporary and historical puppets from around the world are displayed in this former eighteenth-century convent and demonstrated in a well-laid-out museum. Highlights include shadow puppets from Turkey and Indonesia, string marionettes, Punch and Judy-style puppets and almost life-sized, faintly disturbing modern figures by Portuguese puppeteer Helena Vaz, which are anything but cute. There are also video displays and projections, while the final room exhibits Wallace and Gromit-style plasticine

SANTOS DISTRICT

figures with demonstrations on how they are manipulated for films.

SANTOS

MAP P.75, POCKET MAP G7

Santos was traditionally a run-down riverside area of factories and warehouses where people only ventured after dark because of its nightclubs. Over the years, artists and designers moved into the inexpensive and expansive warehouse spaces, and now Santos has a reputation as the city's designer heartland. Its riverside streets are not particularly alluring, but you can see many of the country's top designers showcasing their products in various shops and galleries – the last Thursday of each month has an open day with exhibitions and street entertainment. Fashionable bars and restaurants have followed in their wake, though much of the upper district remains fairly traditional – and the area around the Museu da Marioneta retains an earthy, villagey feel to its cobbled backstreets.

Shops

GALERIA REVERSO

Rua da Esperança 59–61 ☎ 213 951 407.
Mon 2–6pm, Tues–Fri 11am–7pm. MAP P.75,
POCKET MAP H7

Jewellery workshop and
gallery managed by well-
known Portuguese designer
Paula Crespo, whose
big, heavy jewellery is
eye-catching. International
designers also feature, many
using unusual materials such
as rubber and wood, though
to buy anything you'll need a
deep purse.

PARIS:SETE

Largo de Santos 14d ☎ 213 933 170.
Mon–Fri 10am–7.30pm, Sat 10.30am–2pm &
3–7pm. MAP P.75, POCKET MAP H7

Bright, white space selling
designer furniture and curios,
with heavyweight names such
as Charles and Ray Eames and
Frank Gehry behind some of
them.

Restaurants

GUARDA MOR

Rua do Guara Mor 8 ☎ 213 928 663. Tues–Fri
12.30–3pm & 7.30–11pm, Sat 7.30–11pm.
MAP P.75, POCKET MAP G7

One of Santos' more local
options serving great, inexpensive dishes such as *pataniscas
de bacalhau* (dried cod cakes),
açorda de gambas (prawns in
bread sauce) and *gambas fritas
com limão* (prawns fried in
lemon). Mains from €10.

PICANHA

Rua das Janelas Verdes 96 ☎ 213 975 401.
Mon–Fri 12.45–3pm & 7.45–11.30pm, Sat &
Sun 7.45–11.30pm. MAP P.75, POCKET MAP G8

This ornately tiled restaurant
specializes in *picanha* (strips of
beef in garlic sauce) accompanied by black-eyed beans,
salad and potatoes. Great if
this appeals to you, since for a
fixed-price of around €15 you
can eat as much of the stuff as
you want; otherwise forget it, as
it's all that's on offer.

TÚNEL DE SANTOS

Largo de Santos 1 ☎ 912 151 850. Mon–Sat
8am–10pm. MAP P.75, POCKET MAP G7

Lively, modern café-restaurant
with brick-vaulted ceilings
and outdoor seating facing
the square, attracting a young
crowd for inexpensive grills,
snacks and salads.

VARINA DA MADRAGOA

Rua das Madres 34 ☎ 213 965 533.
Tues–Fri 12.30–3.30pm & 7–11.30pm, Sat
7.30–11.30pm. MAP P.75, POCKET MAP G7

A delightfully simple local that
has hosted the likes of fomer
US President Jimmy Carter and
Portuguese PM José Socrates
– and it's easy to see why they
liked it: a lovely, traditional
restaurant with grape-motif
azulejos on the walls and a
menu featuring dishes such
as *bacalhau*, trout and steaks.
Desserts include a splendid
almond ice cream with hot
chocolate sauce. Around €25
for a full meal.

Cafés

MUSEU NACIONAL DE ARTE ANTIGA CAFÉ

Rua das Janelas Verdes 95 ☎ 213 912 800,
Tues 2–5.30pm, Wed–Sun 10am–5.30pm.
MAP P.75, POCKET MAP G8

There's no need to visit the
museum to use its fantastic
café – go in through the
museum exit opposite Largo
Dr J de Figueiredo and head
to the basement. Lunches
and drinks can be enjoyed
in a superb garden studded
with statues and overlooking
Lisbon's docks.

Bars and clubs

ESTADO LIQUIDO

Largo de Santos 5 ☎ 213 972 022, Ⓦ www
.estadoliquido.com. Sun–Thurs 8pm–2am, Fri
& Sat 8pm–4am. MAP P.75, POCKET MAP G7

Right on Santos' main square,
this sushi-restaurant with
attached bar/club has a roomy
feel despite its popularity with
the kids lured by the prominent
club DJs. Easy-going door
policy and efficient service.

KREMLIN

Escadinhas da Praia 5 ☎ 213 957101, Ⓦ www
.grupo-k.pt. Tues–Sat midnight–10am. MAP
P.75, POCKET MAP G7

The tough door policy, based
on its reputation as one of
the city's most fashionable
nightspots, has put off many
old-hand clubbers. However,
it's still packed with flash,
young, raving Lisboetas. It's
best to come after 2am.

LE CHAT

Jardim 9 de Abril. ☎ 966 537 387. Mon–Wed
& Sun noon–midnight, Thurs–Sat noon–3am.
MAP P.75, POCKET MAP F8.

A modern, glass-sided café-bar
adjacent to the Museu Nacional
de Arte Antiga, *Le Chat* has
a terrific terrace which gazes
over the docks and Ponte 25 de
Abril. Great at any time of the
day, it's a particularly fine spot
for a cocktail or sundowner.

PERÓLA

Calçada Ribeiro de Santos 25 ☎ 966 439
164. Tues–Sun 10pm–3am. MAP P.75, POCKET
MAP G7

A small local bar given a
fashionable makeover, with
table football to play and a little
back dining area. Most hole up
in the front room for inexpensive drinks and good music
before moving on to nearby
Kapital or *Kremlin*.

KREMLIN

Fado and live music

B.LEZA

Largo Conde de Barão 50 ☎ 213 963 735.
Tues–Sun 8pm–6am. MAP P.75, POCKET MAP H7

There's live African music
most nights in this wonderful
sixteenth-century building,
with plenty of space to dance,
tables to relax at, and Cape
Verdean food.

O SENHOR VINHO

Rua do Meio à Lapa 18 ☎ 213 972 681,
Ⓦ www.srvinho.com. Mon–Sat 7.30pm–2am.
MAP P.75, POCKET MAP G7

In the fashionable Madragoa
district, this famous fado
club features some of the best
singers in Portugal, hence the
high prices (usually around
€50 a head). Reservations are
advised, and remember – it's
simply not done to talk during
a performance!

Alcântara and the docks

Loomed over by the enormous Ponte 25 de Abril suspension bridge, Alcântara has a decidedly industrial hue, with a tangle of flyovers and cranes from the docks dominating the skyline. The area is well known for its nightlife, thanks mainly to its dockside warehouse conversions that shelter cafés, restaurants and clubs. It also hosts a couple of fine museums, both tipping their hats to Portugal's historic links with the Far East and there's an attractive riverside promenade. To get to the docks, take a train from Cais do Sodré to Alcântara-Mar or tram #15.

DOCA DE ALCÂNTARA

MAP BELOW, POCKET MAP F8

The earthy Doca de Alcântara remains the city's main harbour. After dark, the boat-bars and warehouse conversions come into their own; its clubs and bars attract an older, more moneyed crowd compared to the trendy Bairro Alto set who wouldn't be seen dead in these parts.

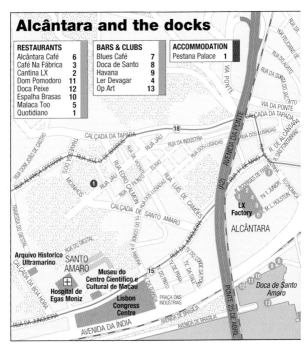

Alcântara and the docks

RESTAURANTS		BARS & CLUBS		ACCOMMODATION	
Alcântara Café	6	Blues Café	7	Pestana Palace	1
Café Na Fábrica	3	Doca de Santo	8		
Cantina LX	2	Havana	9		
Dom Pomodoro	11	Ler Devagar	4		
Doca Peixe	12	Op Art	13		
Espalha Brasas	10				
Malaca Too	5				
Quotidiano	1				

MUSEU DO ORIENTE

Avenida Brasília ☎ 213 585 200, Ⓦ www
.museudooriente.pt. Tues–Sun 10am–6pm,
late opening Fri until 10pm. €5, free Fri
6–10pm. MAP BELOW, POCKET MAP E8

Owned by the powerful Orient
Foundation, this spacious
museum traces the cultural
links that Portugal has built
up with its former colonies in
Macao, India, East Timor and
other Asian countries. Housed
in an enormous 1930s *Estado
Novo* building, highlights of
the extensive collection include
valuable nineteenth-century
Chinese porcelain, an amazing
array of seventeenth-century
Chinese snuff boxes and, from
the same century, Japanese
armour and entire carved
pillars from Goa. The top floor
is given over to displays on the
Gods of Asia, featuring a bright
collection of religious costumes
and shrines used in Bali and

MUSEU DO ORIENTE

Vietnam together with Taoist
altars, statues of Buddha, some
fine Japanese Shinto masks and
Indonesian shadow puppets.
Vivid images of Hindu gods
Shiva, Ganesh the elephant
god and Kali the demon are
counterbalanced by some lovely
Thai amulets. There is also a
decent top-floor restaurant.

ALCÂNTARA AND THE DOCKS

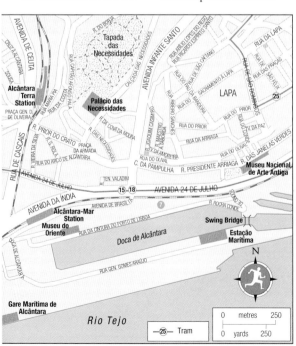

DOCA DE SANTO AMARO

MAP P.80–81, POCKET MAP D9

Just west of the Doca de Alcântara lies the more intimate
Doca de Santo Amaro, nestling
right under the humming
traffic and rattling trains
crossing Ponte 25 de Abril.
This small, almost completely
enclosed marina is filled with
bobbing sailing boats and
lined with tastefully converted
warehouses. Its international
cafés and restaurants are
pricier than usual for Lisbon
but the constant comings and
goings of the Tejo provide
plenty of free entertainment.
Leaving Doca de Santo Amaro
at its western side, you can
pick up a pleasant riverside
path that leads all the way
to Belém (see p.86), twenty
minutes' walk away.

PONTE 25 DE ABRIL

MAP P.80–81, POCKET MAP D9

Resembling the Golden Gate
bridge in San Francisco, the
hugely impressive Ponte 25
de Abril was opened in 1966
as a vital link between Lisbon
and the southern banks of the
Tejo. Around 2.3km in length,
the main bridge rises to 70m
above the river, though its
main pillars are nearly 200m
tall. It was originally named
Ponte de Salazar after the
dictatorial prime minister
who ruled Portugal with an
iron fist from 1932 to 1968,
but took its present name to
mark the date of the revolution that overthrew Salazar's
regime in 1974. You'll pass
over it if you take a bus or train
south of the Tejo. Driving over
it is pretty hairy, especially

on the lane made up of wire mesh (it allows the bridge to expand) – it is both skiddy and see-through.

MUSEU DO CENTRO CIENTÍFICO E CULTURAL DE MACAU

Rua da Junqueira 30 ☎ 213 617 570, ⓦ www
.cccm.mctes.pt. Tues–Sun 10am–6pm. €3.50,
free Sun 10am–2pm. MAP P.80–81, POCKET MAP C9

This attractively laid-out museum is dedicated to Portugal's historical trading links with the Orient and, specifically, its former colony of Macao, which was handed back to Chinese rule in 1999. There are model boats and audio displays detailing early sea voyages, as well as various historic journals and artefacts, including a seventeenth-century portable wooden altar, used by travelling clergymen. Upstairs, exhibitions of Chinese art from the sixteenth to the nineteenth centuries show off ornate collections of porcelain, silverware and applied art, most notably an impressive array of opium pipes and ivory boxes.

LX FACTORY

Rua Rodrigues Faria 103 ☎ 213 143 399, ⓦ www
.lxfactory.com. MAP P.80–81, POCKET MAP D8

Below Ponte 25 de Abril, this former industrial estate is

LER DEVAGAR, LX FACTORY

now the place to test Lisbon's creative pulse. The factories and warehouses have turned into a mini district of workshops and studios for the city's go-getters, along with a series of superb boutiques, shops and cafés set in fashionably run-down urban spaces. Highlights include bookshop *Ler Devagar* (see p.85) and restaurant *Malaca Too* (see p.84). Sunday is a good time to visit, with a lively flea market (noon–7pm) and many places open for brunch. Check the website for LX Factory's Open Days, when there are shows, live music and film screenings.

Ethnic Lisbon

When Africans sailed on the Tejo in the fifteenth century, most would have first glimpsed Lisbon as they passed Alcântara on slave ships during Portugal's ruthless maritime explorations. Today, over 120,000 people of African and Asian descent live in the Greater Lisbon area, most hailing originally from Portugal's former colonies – Cape Verde, Angola, Mozambique, Brazil, Goa and Macao. The 1974 revolution and subsequent independence of the former colonies saw another wave of immigrants settle in the capital. Nowadays African and Brazilian culture permeate Lisbon life, influencing its music, food, television and street slang. Most Lisboetas are rightly proud of their cosmopolitan city, although, inevitably, racism persists and few from ethnic minorities have managed to break through the glass ceiling to the top jobs.

DOM POMODORO

Restaurants

ALCÂNTARA CAFÉ

Rua Maria Luísa Holstein 15 ☎ 213 621 226.
Daily 8pm–3am. MAP P.80–81, POCKET MAP D8

Stunning, if pricey, designer
bar-restaurant, blending
industrial steel pillars with
stylish decor. The food includes
prawns in lemon sauce, goat's
cheese salad and an array of
fish dishes. Book ahead.

CAFÉ NA FÁBRICA

LX Factory, Rua Rodrigues Faria 103 ☎ 967
382 848. Mon–Fri 9.30am–7pm, Sat–Sun
noon–8pm. MAP P.80, POCKET MAP D8.

Set in a small but cosy wooden
warehouse, this arty space is
very popular for lunch, with
wraps, quiches, baguettes and
salads from around €6.50. There
are also a few outdoor tables.

CANTINA LX

LX Factory, Rua Rodrigues Faria 103
☎ 213 628 239. Mon 9.30am–3pm, Tues–Fri
9am–11pm, Sat noon–11pm. MAP P.80–81,
POCKET MAP D8

This is the place to be seen in
the LX Factory complex (see
p.83), with bench-like tables in
a spacious former warehouse.
Great breakfasts, snacks and
daily specials which usually
focus on healthy salads from
around €10.

DOM POMODORO

Armazém 13, Doca de Santo Amaro ☎ 213
909 353. Daily noon–2am. MAP P.80–81, POCKET
MAP D9

The best place to get an
inexpensive meal in the docks,
albeit Italian, with good-value
and tasty pasta, pizza and the
like from €9. Attractive seating
on two floors and outdoor
waterside tables.

DOCA PEIXE

Armazém 14, Doca de Santo Amaro ☎ 213
973 556. Daily 12.30pm–11.30pm. MAP P.80–81,
POCKET MAP D9

You'll need a deep wallet to eat
at this fish restaurant (mains
from €15), but with a counter
groaning under the weight
of fresh fish, you won't leave
disappointed. They also serve
a great fish curry and sublime
lobster tagliatelle.

ESPALHA BRASAS

Armazém 12, Doca de Santo Amaro ☎ 213
962 059. Mon–Sat noon–4am. MAP P.80–81,
POCKET MAP D9

Superb grilled meats, tiger
prawns and fish kebabs can be
enjoyed at the riverside tables,
or head for the bright upstairs
room, which offers great views
over the river. Daily specials
around €14.

MALACA TOO

LX Factory, Rua Rodrigues Faria 103 ☎ 213
477 082. Daily noon–midnight. MAP P.80, POCKET
MAP D8.

This fantastic space has tables
wedged between giant old
printing presses – a surprising
backdrop for fresh, oriental
cuisine ranging from wanton

soups and green curries to fresh fish, from around €14.

QUOTIDIANO

Largo das Fontainhas 7. ☎ 211 571 690. Mon–Thurs noon–midnight, Fri &, Sat noon–2am. MAP P.80–81, POCKET MAP D8

Modern and alluring café-restaurant – all Nordic stripped pine and white walls – on a lively square. The menu features a range of quality cakes, pastries, drinks and reasonably priced dishes of the day (under €9); packed at lunchtime so arrive early.

Bars and clubs

BLUES CAFÉ

Rua da Cintura do Porto de Lisboa ☎ 213 957 085. Tues–Wed 8pm–2am, Thurs–Sat 8pm–6am. MAP P.80–81, POCKET MAP F8

Lisbon's only blues club occupies a converted dockside warehouse. There's pricey international food served in the restaurant until 12.30am, live music on Mondays and Thursdays, and club nights with the latest dance music from Thursday to Saturday from midnight.

CANTINA LX

DOCA DE SANTO

Armazém CP, Doca de Santo Amaro ☎ 213 963 535. Mon–Thurs 12.30pm–1am, Fri–Sun 12.30pm–4am. MAP P.80–81, POCKET MAP D8

Though it's located slightly away from the river, this palm-fringed venue is worth seeking out; there's an enticing cocktail bar on the esplanade, while the restaurant inside serves well-priced modern Portuguese food (grilled fish and meats with pasta or couscous). From €13.

HAVANA

Armazém 5, Doca de Santo Amaro ☎ 213 979 893, ⓦ www.havana.com.pt. Daily noon–6am. MAP P.80–81, POCKET MAP D9

Cuban-themed music bar with wicker chairs and Latin music. It also does moderately priced salads and snacks.

LER DEVAGAR

LX Factory, Rua Rodrigues Faria 103 ☎ 213 259 992, ⓦ www.lerdevagar.com. Mon–Thurs noon–midnight, Fri–Sat noon–2am, Sun noon–10pm. MAP P.80, POCKET MAP D8.

Primarily a wonderful bookshop, with shelves reaching to the heavens of an old printing press, this also has a corner café-bar, a great place to sample Portuguese wines and local cheeses including soft Nisa eand mountain cheeses from €3–4.

OP ART

Doca de Santo Amaro ☎ 213 956 797 ⓦ www .opartcafe.com. Tues–Fri & Sun 3pm–2am. Sat 3pm–6am. MAP P.80–81, POCKET MAP D9

Set in splendid isolation on the fringes of the Tejo, this small glass pavilion morphs from a minimalist restaurant serving moderately priced grills into a groovy evening bar. After dusk, the volume pumps up and it turns into more of a club. In summer, you can sprawl on the dockside beanbags and gaze over the river.

Belém and Ajuda

With its maritime history and attractive riverside location, Belém (pronounced ber-layng) is understandably one of Lisbon's most popular suburbs. It was from Belém that Vasco da Gama famously set sail for India in 1497 and returned a year later. The monastery subsequently built here – the Mosteiro dos Jerónimos – stands as a testament to his triumphant discovery of a sea route to the Orient, which initiated the beginning of a Portuguese golden age. Along with the monastery and the landmark Torre de Belém, the suburb boasts a group of small museums including the fantastic Berardo Collection of modern art. Just to the north-east of Belém is Ajuda, famed for its palace and ancient botanical gardens. Higher still lies the extensive parkland of Monsanto, Lisbon's largest green space.

PRAÇA DO IMPÉRIO

MAP P.88–89, POCKET MAP C4

The formal gardens and walkways that make up Praça do Império are laid out over Belém's former beach. It's a popular spot, especially on Saturday mornings, when there are often weddings taking place at the monastery, whose photo-calls invariably spill out into the square. The attractive seventeenth-century buildings along Rua Vieira Portuense are now mostly restaurants with outdoor seating; as a rule, the further east you head, the better value they become.

JARDIM DO ULTRAMAR AND PRESIDÊNCIA DA REPÚBLICA

Garden entrance on Calçada do Galvão. Daily May–Sept 10am–6pm, Oct–April 10am–5pm. €2. MAP P.88–89, POCKET MAP C4

The leafy Jardim do Ultramar is an oasis of hothouses, ponds and towering palms, a lovely place for a shady walk. In the southeastern corner lies the Portuguese President's official residence, the pink Presidência da República, which opens its state rooms for guided visits on weekends (entrance on Praça Afonso de Albuquerque, Sat 11am–4pm, Sun 2.30–4pm, €5; Ⓦ www.museu.presidencia.pt).

Belém transport

You can reach Belém on tram #15 (signed Algés), which runs from Praça da Figueira via Praça do Comércio and Cais do Sodré (20min). You can also take a 45-minute Yellowbus minibus tour (9.30am–5pm; May–Oct every 30min; Nov–April every hour Mon–Fri, every 30min Sat & Sun; €10), departing from in front of the Mosteiro dos Jerónimos, which goes up to the palace at Ajuda and back via the Torre de Belém. Alternatively, hire bikes (Mon–Fri noon–8pm, Sat & Sun 10am–8pm, €4.50/1hr; Ⓦ www.belembike .com) from a kiosk just east of the Museu da Electricidade (see p.91)

MOSTEIRO DOS JERÓNIMOS

MUSEU DE ARTE POPULAR

Avenida de Brasília ☎ 213 011 282, ⓦ www
.map.imc-ip.pt. Wed–Sun 10am–1pm &
2pm–6pm, €2. Free Sun 10am–1pm. MAP P.88,
POCKET MAP B5.

In a space which feels slightly
too large for its exhibits, this
charming museum chronicles
Portugal's folk art, from
beautiful wood and cork toys to
ceramics, rugs and fascinating
traditional costumes, including
amazing cloaks from the Trás-
os-Montes region.

MOSTEIRO DOS JERÓNIMOS

Praça do Império ☎ 213 620 034, ⓦ www
.mosteirojeronimos.pt. Daily: May–Sept
10am–6pm; Oct–April 10am–5pm; restricted
access on Sat mornings and during Mass.
Free. MAP P.88–89, POCKET MAP C4.

A UNESCO World Heritage
site, the Mosteiro dos
Jerónimos is Portugal's most
successful achievement of
Manueline architecture.
Construction began in 1502,
the result of a vow that Dom
Manuel had made to the
Virgin that he would build a
monastery should Vasco da
Gama return successfully from
his trip to India. The design
was largely the brainchild of
Diogo de Boitaca, perhaps the
originator of the Manueline

style, and João de Castilho,
a Spaniard who took charge
of construction from around
1517. Castilho designed the
main entrance – an arch
decorated with a complex
hierarchy of figures clustered
around Henry the Navigator.
Just inside the entrance lie the
stone tombs of **Vasco da Gama**
(1468–1523) and the great poet
and recorder of the discoveries,
Luís de Camões (1527–70).

The breathtaking sense of
space inside the church places
it among the greatest triumphs
of European Gothic while its
rich Manueline detail provides
a deliberate contrast. The six
central columns resemble giant
palm trunks, growing both into
and from the branches of the
delicate rib-vaulting.

Equally stunning are the
beautifully vaulted **cloisters**
(€7, free Sun 10am–2pm). The
rounded corner canopies and
elegant twisting arches lend a
wave-like, undulating appearance to the whole structure,
a conceit extended by the
typically Manueline motifs of
ropes, anchors and the sea.
Round the edges of the cloisters
you can still see twelve niches
where pilgrims and sailors
stopped for confessionals.

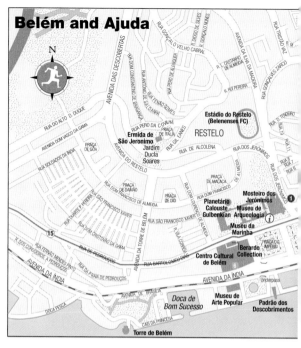

Belém and Ajuda

MUSEU DE ARQUEOLOGIA

Praça do Império ☎ 213 620 000, ⓦ www
.mnarqueologia-ipmuseus.pt.Tues–Sun
10am–6pm. €5. free Sun 10am–2pm. MAP
ABOVE, POCKET MAP C4

Housed in a neo-Manueline
extension to the monastery
added in 1850, the archeology
museum has a small section
on Egyptian antiquities dating
from 6000 BC, but concentrates
on Portuguese archeological
finds. It's a sparse collection
reprieved by coins and jewellery through the ages, and a
few fine Roman mosaics.

MUSEU DA MARINHA

Praça do Império ☎ 213 620 019, ⓦ www
.museumarinha.pt. Tues–Sun: May–Sept
10am–6pm; Oct–April 10am–5pm. €4. MAP
ABOVE, POCKET MAP B4

In the west wing of the monastery extension is an absorbing
and gargantuan maritime
museum, packed not only
with models of ships, naval
uniforms and artefacts from
Portugal's oriental colonies,
but also with real vessels –
among them fishing boats and
sumptuous state barges, plus
early seaplanes. Much of the
collection comes from that of
King Luís I (1861–1889), a keen
oceanographer.

CENTRO CULTURAL DE BELÉM

Praça do Império ☎ 213 612 400, ⓦ www.ccb
.pt. MAP ABOVE. POCKET MAP B4

The stylish, modern, pink
marble Centro Cultural
de Belém was built to host
Lisbon's 1992 presidency of
the European Union. It's now
one of the city's main cultural
centres, containing the Berardo
Collection (see p.89) and
hosting regular photography
and art exhibitions, as well as
concerts and shows.

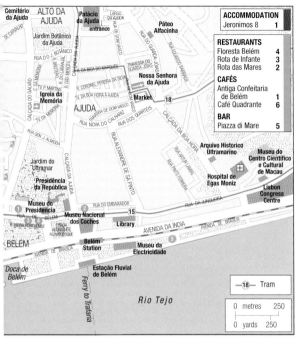

BERARDO COLLECTION

Entrance via Centro Cultural de Belém, Praça do Império ☏ 213 612 878, ✆ www .museuberardo.pt. Daily 10am–7pm. Free. MAP ABOVE, POCKET MAP B4

As impressive as Belém's historical monuments is this unique collection of modern art amassed by wealthy Madeiran Joe Berardo, Portugal's answer to Charles Saatchi or François Pinault. You can enjoy some of the world's top modern artists, though not all of the vast collection is on display at the same time. Depending on when you visit, you may see Eric Fischl's giant panels of sunbathers; Andy Warhol's distinctive *Judy Garland*; and Chris Ofili's *Adoration of Captain Shit*, made with genuine dung. Portugal's Paula Rego is well represented – *The Past and Present* and *The*

Barn are particularly strong. Francis Bacon, David Hockney, Picasso, Míro, Man Ray, Max Ernst and Mark Rothko also feature, along with various video artists.

JUDY GARLAND BY ANDY WARHOL

PADRÃO DOS DESCOBRIMENTOS

Avenida de Brasília, reached via an underpass beneath the Avenida da Índia ☎213 031 950, Ⓦwww.padraodescobrimentos .egeac.pt. Daily: May–Sept 10am–7pm, Oct–April 10am–6pm. €3. MAP P.88–89, POCKET MAP C5

The Padrão dos Descobrimentos (Monument to the Discoveries) is a 54m-high, caravel-shaped slab of concrete erected in 1960 to commemorate the 500th anniversary of the death of Henry the Navigator. A large and detailed statue of Henry appears at the head of a line of statues that feature King Alfonso V, Luís de Camões, Vasco de Gama and other Portuguese heroes. Inside is a small exhibition space which often features displays on Lisbon's history – the entrance fee also includes a ride in the lift providing fine views of the Tejo and the Torre de Belém. Just in front of the monument, tourists pose on the marble pavement decorated with a map of the world charting the routes taken by the great Portuguese explorers.

TORRE DE BELÉM

☎213 620 034. Tues–Sun: May–Sept 10am–6.30pm; Oct–April 10am–5.30pm. €5, free Sun 10am–2pm. MAP P.88–89, POCKET MAP A5

The Torre de Belém, 500m west of the monastery, was built over the last five years of Dom Manuel's reign (1515–20) to defend the mouth of the Tejo – before an earthquake shifted the river's course in 1777, the tower stood near the middle of the waters. The tower is the country's only example of a building started and completed during the Manueline era (the rest having been adaptations of earlier structures or completed in later years) and has become an iconic symbol of Lisbon.

Its Moorish influence is clear in the delicately arched windows and balconies. Prominent also in the decoration are two great icons of the age: Manuel's personal badge of an armillary sphere (representing the globe); and the cross of the military Order of Christ, once the Templars, who took a major role in all the Portuguese

MUSEU DA ELECTRICIDADE

Avenida de Brasilia ☎ 213 028 190. Tues–Sun 10am–6pm. Free. MAP P.88-89, POCKET MAP D4

The extraordinary red-brick Museu da Electricidade (Electricity Museum) is housed in an early twentieth-century electricity generating station. The highlights include a series of enormous generators, steam turbines and winches; it also hosts regular art and technology exhibitions. From in front of the museum, it is possible to walk the 1.5km along the lawned riverside all the way to the Doca de Santo Amaro one way, or the 1km to central Belém the other way.

PALÁCIO DA AJUDA

Largo da Ajuda ☎213 620 264, ⓦ www .pnajuda.imc-ip.pt. Tram #18 from Praça do Comércio or bus #729 from Belém. Mon, Tues & Thurs–Sun 10am–5.30pm. €5, free Sun 10am–2pm occasionally open eves for classical concerts. MAP P.88-89, POCKET MAP D2

This massive nineteenth-century palace sits on a hillside above Belém. Construction began in 1802, but was left incomplete when João VI and the royal family fled to Brazil to escape Napoleon's invading army in 1807. The original plans were therefore never fulfilled, though the completed section was used as a royal residence after João returned from exile in 1821. The crashingly tasteless decor was commissioned by the nineteenth-century royal, Dona Maria II (João's grand-daughter), and gives an insight into the opulent life the royals lived. The Queen's bedroom comes complete with a polar bearskin rug, while the throne and ballroom are impressive for their sheer size and extravagance. The highly ornate banqueting hall, full of crystal chandeliers is also breathtaking.

conquests. Clamber up the steep internal stairs via a series of bare rooms for great views from the top. When inside, it is also easy to imagine what it was like in the nineteenth century when it was used as a prison, notoriously by Dom Miguel (1828–34), who kept political enemies in the water-logged dungeons.

MUSEU DOS COCHES

Praça Afonso de Albuquerque ☎ 213 610 850, ⓦ www.museudoscoches-ipmuseus.pt. Tues–Sun 10am–6pm, free Sun 10am–2pm. €4. MAP P.88-89, POCKET MAP D4

Recently rehoused in a modern building, the Museu dos Coches (coach museum) was originally opened in 1905 and contains one of the largest collections of carriages and saddlery in the world. Heavily gilded and sometimes beautifully painted, the coaches date from the sixteenth to nineteenth centuries. From the same period are sedan chairs, children's buggies and a very rare sixteenth-century coach designed for King Felipe I (Spain's King Philip II).

PÁTEO ALFACINHA

JARDIM BOTÂNICO DA AJUDA

Entrance on Calçada da Ajuda ☎ 213 622
503 🌐 www.jardimbotanicodaajuda.com. Daily
May–Sept 9am–8pm, Oct–April 9am–7pm. €2.
MAP P.88-89, POCKET MAP C2

A classic example of formal
Portuguese gardening, this
is one of the city's oldest and
most interesting botanical
gardens. Commissioned by the
Marquês de Pombal and laid
out in 1768, it was owned by
the royal family until the birth
of the Republic in 1910, then
substantially restored in the
1990s. The garden is divided
into eight parts planted with
plant species from around the
world, all arranged around a
system of terraces, statues and
fountains, much of it offering
lovely views over the river.

PÁTEO ALFACINHA

Rua do Guarda Jóias 44 ☎ 213 628 258. MAP
P.88-89, POCKET MAP D2

Just five minutes' walk from
the Palácio da Ajuda, it
is worth seeking out this
highly picturesque *páteo* – a
renovated cluster of traditional nineteenth-century
Lisbon houses gathered round
a central patio. These were
common in the days when
relatively humble families lived
in tight-knit communities who
looked after and traded with
each other. Today the houses
only come alive for special
events and private parties, often
laid on at weekends, though
there is a permanent restaurant,
Sala Menina, which does good-
value grills.

PARQUE FLORESTAL DE MONSANTO

Bus #729. MAP P.88-89, POCKET MAP E2

The extensive hillside Parque
Florestal de Monsanto – home
to the city's main and well-
equipped campsite (🌐 www.
campings.net) – is known as
"Lisbon's lungs" though its
other main attraction used to
be the prostitutes who worked
here until the Mayor of Lisbon
bought a house nearby in
2003. Suddenly the park was
given a new lease of life and
the hookers have since been
replaced by horse-and-trap
rides to its splendid viewpoints.
At weekends in summer the
whole area is completely traffic-
free and pop concerts are often
laid on, usually free of charge.

Restaurants

FLORESTA BELÉM

Praça Afonso de Albuquerque 1 ☏ 213 636 307 Tues–Sat noon–4pm & 6.30pm–midnight, Sun noon–4pm. MAP P.88-89, POCKET MAP C4

On the corner with Rua Vieira Portuense, this attracts a largely Portuguese clientele, especially for lunch at the weekend. Great salads, grills and fresh fish from around €7, served inside or on a sunny outdoor terrace.

ROTA DO INFANTE

Rua Vieira Portuense 10–14 ☏ 213 646 787. Daily noon–3pm & 7.30–11pm, closed Mon Oct–April. MAP P.88-89, POCKET MAP C4

One of the best-value places in this pretty row of buildings facing the greenery of Praça do Império. Decently priced fish and meat from around €8, with outdoor seats under fragrant orange trees.

ROTA DAS MARES

Rua da Junqueira 506. ☏ 213 642 857. Tues–Sun 10am–10pm. MAP P.88-89, POCKET MAP D4

Just far enough from the main sights to keep prices sensible, this spacious restaurant bustles at weekends with locals filling up with no-nonsense grills and fish; a full meal with wine should be under €15.

Cafés

ANTIGA CONFEITARIA DE BELÉM

Rua de Belém 84–92. Daily 8am–midnight, Oct–May closes 11pm. MAP P.88-89, POCKET MAP C4

No visit to Belém is complete without a coffee and hot *pastel de nata* (custard-cream tart) liberally sprinkled with *canela* (cinnamon) in this cavernous, tiled pastry shop and café, which has been serving them up since 1837. The place positively heaves, especially at weekends, but there's usually space to sit down in its warren of rooms.

CAFÉ QUADRANTE

Centro Cultural de Belém. Daily 10am–10pm, closes 9pm on Sat & Sun from Oct–April. MAP P.88-89, POCKET MAP B4

Part of the Belém Cultural Centre, this café offers good-value self-service food from two counters. The best place to enjoy coffee and snacks is on the outdoor terrace by the roof gardens, overlooking the river. It's so popular with students that they are forbidden from studying here at mealtimes.

Bars

PIAZZA DI MARE

Avenida Brasília, Pavilhão Poente ☏ 213 624 235. Daily 11am–11pm. MAP P.88-89, POCKET MAP B9

Though you may baulk at paying €15 or more for the pasta and pizza dishes, this upmarket Italian restaurant also has an excellent riverside café-bar area where anyone can enjoy a modestly priced snack or drink facing the river.

ANTIGA CONFEITARIA DE BELÉM

Avenida, Parque Eduardo VII and the Gulbenkian

Lisbon's main avenue, Avenida da Liberdade (simply known as "Avenida"), links the centre with its principal park, Parque Eduardo VII, best known for its views and enormous hothouses. The avenue, together with its side streets, was once home to statesmen and public figures. On its western side is the historic Praça das Amoreiras, the finishing point of the massive Águas Livres aqueduct. Here you'll find the Fundação Arpad Siznes-Viera da Silva, a collection of works by two artists heavily influenced by Lisbon. Northwest of the park, the Fundação Calouste Gulbenkian is undoubtedly Portugal's premier cultural centre, featuring one of Europe's richest art collections. Art-lovers have a further attraction to the east, where you can view the historic paintings and objects in the Casa Museu Dr Anastácio Gonçalves. Just north of here is the bullring at Campo Pequeno, while east lies the city's zoo.

AVENIDA DA LIBERDADE

MAP P.96-97, POCKET MAP J5

The 1.3km, palm-lined Avenida da Liberdade is still much as poet Fernando Pessoa described it: "the finest artery in Lisbon… full of trees …small gardens, ponds, fountains, cascades and statues". It was laid out in 1882 as the city's main north-south avenue, and has several appealing outdoor cafés under the shade of trees that help cushion the

roar of the passing traffic. Some of the avenue's original nineteenth-century mansions remain, though most have been replaced by modern buildings. The upper end of the avenue houses many of the city's designer shops and ends in a swirl of traffic at the landmark roundabout of Praça Marquês de Pombal, also known as Rotunda.

PARQUE MAYER

MAP P.96–97, POCKET MAP J5

Opened in 1922 as an "entertainment precinct" when theatres were all the rage, the rundown Parque Mayer is still one of the capital's main destinations for theatregoers, though has long been earmarked for substantial renovation. This may lead to the controversial demolishing of the listed **Teatro Capitólio** – not the most handsome of theatres, but its concrete angular form is the country's first great Modernist structure.

CASA MUSEU MEDEIROS E ALMEIDA

Rua Rosa Araújo 41 ☎ 213 547 892. 🌐 www .casa-museumedeirosealmeida.pt. Mon–Fri 1–5.30pm, Sat 10am–5.30pm. €5, free Sat 10am–1pm. MAP P.96–97, POCKET MAP H5

The Fundação Medeiros e Almeida was the home of the industrialist, philanthropist and art collector António Medeiros until his death in 1986. Today it serves as a showcase for his priceless series of artefacts. His collection of 225 Chinese porcelain items (some 2000 years old), sixteenth- to nineteenth-century watches, and English and Portuguese silverware are considered the most valuable in the world. Other highlights include glorious eighteenth-century azulejos in the Sala de Lago,

MURAL, PARQUE MAYER

a room complete with large water fountains; and a rare seventeenth-century clock, made for Queen Catherine of Bragança and mentioned by Samuel Pepys in his diary.

PRAÇA DAS AMOREIRAS

MAP P.96–97, POCKET MAP G5

One of Lisbon's most tranquil squares, Praça das Amoreiras – complete with kids' play area – is dominated on its western side by the Águas Livres aqueduct (see p.98), with a chapel wedged into its arches.

On the south side the **Mãe d'Água** cistern (☎ 218 135 522; Mon–Sat 10am–6pm; €3) marks the end of the line for the aqueduct. Built between 1746 and 1834, the castellated stone building contains a reservoir that once supplied the city. The structure nowadays hosts occasional temporary art exhibitions. Head to the back where there are stairs leading on to the roof for great views over the city. Back on the square, the little kiosk café is a popular spot for a coffee or beer and also hosts occasional art exhibits.

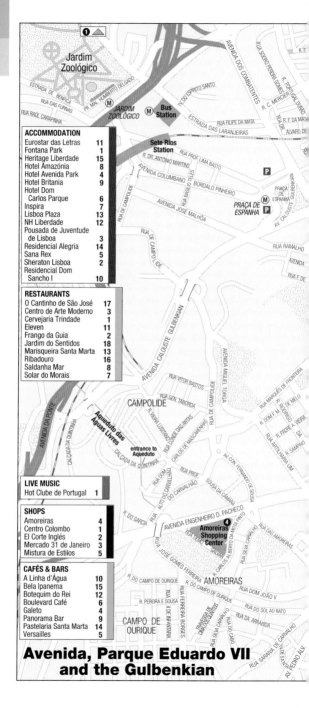

Avenida, Parque Eduardo VII and the Gulbenkian

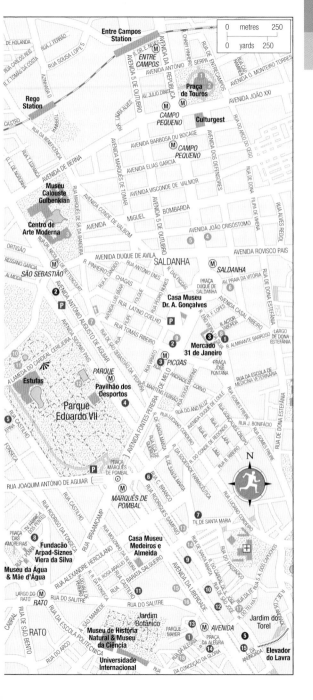

FUNDAÇÃO ARPAD SIZNES-VIERA DA SILVA

Praça das Amoreiras 56–58 ☎ 213 880 044, ⓦ www.fasvs.pt. Mon–Sun 10am–6pm. €4, free Sun 10am–6pm. MAP P.96–97, POCKET MAP G5

The Fundação Arpad Siznes-Viera da Silva is a small but highly appealing gallery dedicated to the works of two painters and the artists who have been influenced by them. Arpad Siznes (1897–1985) was a Hungarian-born artist and friend of Henri Matisse and Pierre Bonnard, amongst others. While in Paris in 1928 he met the Portuguese artist Maria Helena Viera da Silva (1908–92), whose work was influenced by the surrealism of Joan Miró and Max Ernst, both of whom she was good friends with. Siznes and Viera da Silva married in 1930 and, in 1936, both exhibited in Lisbon, where they briefly lived, before eventually settling in France. The foundation shows the development of the artists' works, with Viera da Silva's more abstract, subdued paintings contrasting with flamboyant Siznes, some of whose paintings show the clear influence of Miró.

AQUEDUTO DAS ÁGUAS LIVRES

Entrance on Calçada da Quintinha 6 ☎ 218 100 215. March–Oct Mon–Sat 10am–6pm. €3. Bus #718 from Amoreiras. MAP P.96–97, POCKET MAP F4

The towering Aqueduto das Águas Livres (Free Waters Aqueduct) was opened in 1748, bringing a reliable source of safe drinking water to the city for the first time. Stretching for 60km (most of it underground), the aqueduct stood firm during the 1755 earthquake though it later gained a more notorious reputation thanks to one Diogo Alves, a nineteenth-century serial killer who threw his victims off the top – a seventy-metre drop. It is possible to walk across a 1.5km section of the aqueduct though you'll need a head for heights. The walkable section is accessed off a quiet residential street through a small park in Campolide, 1km north of Praça das Amoreiras.

AQUEDUTO DAS ÁGUAS LIVRES

FUNDAÇÃO CALOUSTE GULBENKIAN

☎ 217 823 000, ⓦ www.gulbenkian.org. MAP P.96–97, POCKET MAP H2

Set in extensive grounds, the Fundação Calouste Gulbenkian was set up by the Armenian oil magnate Calouste Gulbenkian (see box p.99) whose legendary art-market coups included the acquisition of works from the Hermitage in St Petersburg. Today the Gulbenkian Foundation has a multi-million dollar budget sufficient to finance work in all spheres of Portuguese cultural life. In this low-rise 1960s complex alone, it runs an orchestra, three concert halls and an attractive open-air amphitheatre.

MUSEU CALOUSTE GULBENKIAN

Avenida de Berna 45a ☏ 217 823 000, ⓦ www
.gulbenkian.pt. Tues–Sun 10am–5.45pm. €4,
free Sun, combined ticket with Centro de Arte
Moderna €7. MAP P.96–97, POCKET MAP H2

The Museu Calouste Gulbenkian covers virtually every
phase of Eastern and Western
art. The small Egyptian room
displays art from the Old
Kingdom (c.2700 BC) up to the
Roman period. Fine Roman
statues, silver and glass, and
gold jewellery from ancient
Greece follow. The Islamic arts
are magnificently represented
by a variety of ornamental
texts, opulently woven carpets,
glassware and Turkish tiles.
There is also porcelain from
China, and beautiful Japanese
prints and lacquer-work.

European art includes work
from all the major schools.
The seventeenth-century
collection yields Peter Paul
Rubens' graphic *The Love
of the Centaurs* (1635) and
Rembrandt's *Figure of an Old
Man*. Featured eighteenth-
century works include those
by Jean-Honoré Fragonard and
Thomas Gainsborough – in
particular the stunning *Portrait
of Mrs Lowndes-Stone*. The
big names of nineteenth- to
twentieth-century France
– Manet, Monet, Degas,
Millet and Renoir – are all
represented, along with John
Sargent and Turner's vivid
Wreck of a Transport Ship
(1810). Elsewhere you'll find
Sèvres porcelain and furniture
from the reigns of Louis XV
and Louis XVI. The last room
features an amazing collection of Art Nouveau jewellery
by René Lalique. Don't miss
the fantastical *Peitoral-libélula*
(Dragonfly breastpiece)
brooch, decorated with enamel
work, gold and diamonds.

Calouste Gulbenkian

Calouste Sarkis Gulbenkian (1869–1955) was the Roman Abramovich
of his era, making his millions from oil but investing in the world's
best art rather than footballers. Born of wealthy Armenian parents in
Istanbul in 1869, he followed his father into the oil industry and eventually
moved to England. After the Russian Revolution of 1917 he bought works
from the Leningrad Hermitage. During World War II, his Turkish background
made him unwelcome in Britain and Gulbenkian auctioned himself to
whoever would have him. Portugal bid an aristocratic palace (a marquês was
asked to move out) and tax exemption, to acquire one of the most important
cultural patrons of the century. From 1942 to his death in 1955, he
accumulated one of the best private art collections in the world. His dying
wish was that all of his collection should be displayed in one place, and this
was granted in 1969 with the opening of the Museu Calouste Gulbenkian.

CENTRO DE ARTE MODERNA JOSÉ AZEREDO PERDIGÃO

Main entrance on Rua Dr Nicolau de Bettencourt ☎ 217 823 000, Ⓦ www .gulbenkian.org. Tues–Sun 10am–5.45pm. €4, free Sun, combined ticket with Museu Calouste Gulbenkian €7. MAP P.96–97, POCKET MAP H2

The Centro de Arte Moderna, part of the Gulbenkian foundation (see p.99), features pop art, installations and sculptures – some witty, some baffling, but all thought-provoking. Most of the big names on the twentieth-century Portuguese scene are included, including portraits and sketches by Almada Negreiros (1873–1970), the founder of *modernismo*, the bright Futurist colours of Amadeu de Sousa Cardoso, and works by Paula Rego, one of Portugal's leading contemporary artists, whose *Mãe* (1997) is outstanding. Pieces from major international artists such as David Hockney and Antony Gormley also feature, though these tend to be temporary.

PARQUE EDUARDO VII

MAP P.96–97, POCKET MAP H4

The steep, formally laid-out Parque Eduardo VII was named to honour Britain's King Edward VII when he visited the city in 1903. Its main building is the ornately tiled Pavilhão dos Desportos (Sports Pavilion), which doubles as a concert venue. North of here is the main viewing platform which offers commanding vistas of the city as well as Ferris wheel during the summer months. Another highlight if you have children is the superb Parque Infantil (open daily; free), a play area built round a mock galleon.

Two huge, rambling **estufas** (daily: Estufa Fria April–Sept 9am–7pm; Oct–March 9am–6pm; Estufa Quente closes 30min earlier; €3) lie close by. Set in substantial former basalt quarries, both are filled with tropical plants, pools and endless varieties of palms and cacti. Of the two, the Estufa Quente (the hothouse) has the more exotic plants; the Estufa Fria (the coldhouse) hosts concerts and exhibitions.

Finally, the hilly northern reaches of the park contain an olive grove and a shallow lake which kids splash about in during the heat of the day.

CASA MUSEU DR ANASTÁCIO GONÇALVES

Avda 5 de Outubro 6–8. Entrance on Rua Pinheiro Chagas ☎ 213 540 823, Ⓦ www .cmag-ipmuseus.pt. Tues 2–6pm, Wed–Sun 10am–6pm. €3. MAP P.96–97, POCKET MAP J3

This appealing neo-Romantic building with Art Nouveau touches – including a beautiful stained-glass window – was originally built for painter José Malhoa in 1904, but now holds the exquisite private collection of ophthalmologist

PARQUE EDUARDO VII

Dr Anastácio Gonçalves, who bought the house in the 1930s. Highlights include paintings by Portuguese landscape artist João Vaz and by Malhoa himself, who specialized in historical paintings – his *Dream of Infante Henriques* is a typical example. You'll also find Chinese porcelain from the sixteenth-century Ming dynasty, along with furniture from England, France, Holland and Spain dating from the seventeenth century.

PRAÇA DE TOUROS

Campo Pequeno ☎ 217 998 450 ⓦ www .campopequeno.com. MAP P.96-97, POCKET MAP J1

Built in 1892, the Praça de Touros at Campo Pequeno is an impressive Moorish-style bullring seating nine thousand spectators. The Portuguese *tourada* (bullfight) is not as famous as its Spanish counterpart, but as a spectacle it's marginally preferable, as here the bull isn't killed in the ring, but instead is wrestled to the ground in a genuinely elegant, colourful and skilled display. During the fight, however, the bull is usually injured and slaughtered later in any case. Performances start at around

10pm on Thursday evenings from Easter to September. Surrounded by a ring of lively cafés and restaurants, the bullring also hosts visiting circuses and other events, while beneath is an underground shopping and cinema complex.

JARDIM ZOOLÓGICO

Praça Marechal Humberto Delgado ☎ 217 232 900, ⓦ www.zoolisboa.pt. Daily: March– Sept 10am–8pm; Oct–Feb 10am–6pm. €17, children under 12 €12.50. MAP P.96-97, POCKET MAP E1

Lisbon's Jardim Zoológico was opened in 1884 and makes for an enjoyable excursion. There's a café-lined park area which you can visit for free and see monkeys, crocodiles and parrots. Once inside the zoo proper, a small cable car (daily from 11am until 30min before closing; included in the price) transports you over many of the animals, and there's a well-stocked reptile house (open 11am until 30min before closing) as further diversion. Just by its main gates lies the Animax amusement park (daily 11am–8pm/7pm winter), where kids can load up a card for rides and games to relieve their parents of further euros.

Shops

AMOREIRAS

Avenida Engenheiro Duarte Pacheco 103. Daily 10am–11pm. Bus #758. MAP P.96–97, POCKET MAP F4

Amoreiras, Lisbon's striking, postmodern commercial centre, is a wild fantasy of pink and blue towers sheltering ten cinemas, sixty cafés and restaurants, 250 shops and a hotel. Built in 1985 and designed by adventurous Portuguese architect Tomás Taveira, most of its stores are open daily; Sunday sees the heaviest human traffic, with entire families descending for an afternoon out.

CENTRO COLOMBO

Avenida Lusíada. Most shops daily 9am–midnight. Metro Colégio Militar/Luz. MAP P.96–97, POCKET MAP F1

Iberia's largest shopping centre is almost a town in its own right, with over 400 shops, 65 restaurants and 11 cinema screens. Major stores include FNAC, C&A, Zara, Mango and Toys "R" Us, while the top floor has the usual fast-food outlets

along with a sit-down dining area in the jungle-themed "Cidade Perdida" (Lost City). There is also a "Fun Centre" (daily: noon–midnight) which claims to be Europe's largest covered amusement park, complete with rides, bumper cars, ten-pin bowling and even a roller coaster that whizzes overhead. An additional outdoor area features mini-bungee jumps, a go-kart track and toy car and boat rides.

EL CORTE INGLÊS

Avda António Augusto de Aguiar. Most shops Mon–Sat 10am–10pm. Cinema info on ☎707 232 221. MAP P.96–97, POCKET MAP H3

A giant Spanish department store spread over nine floors, two of which are underground. The basement specializes in gourmet food, with various delis, bakers and a supermarket (closed Sun afternoon), while the upper floors offer a range of stylish goods, including clothes, sports gear, books, CDs and toys. The top floor packs in cafés and restaurants with an outdoor terrace. There's also a fourteen-screen cinema in the basement.

EL CORTE INGLÊS

MERCADO 31 DE JANEIRO

Rua Enginheiro Viera da Silva. Mon–Sat 7am–2pm. MAP P.96–97, POCKET MAP J3

This bustling local market is divided into sections; you'll find a colourful array of fresh fruit, vegetables, spices, fish, flowers and a few crafts.

MISTURA DE ESTILOS

Rua São José 21. Mon–Fri 3–8pm. MAP P.96–97, POCKET MAP J5

This tiny shop sells individually crafted tiles from around €4 – as the name implies, the styles are mixed – from plain patterns to lovely animal motifs – but most are simple, effective and portable.

Restaurants

O CANTINHO DE SÃO JOSÉ

Rua São José 94 ☎ 213 427 866. Mon–Fri & Sun 11am–11pm. MAP P.96–97, POCKET MAP J5

Friendly *tasca* serving generous portions at bargain prices – tuck into a full meal of grilled meat, salmon or other fish with wine and you may get change from €12.

CENTRO DE ARTE MODERNA

Rua Dr Bettencourt, Fundação Calouste Gulbenkian. Tues–Sun 10am–5.45pm. MAP P.96–97, POCKET MAP H2

Join the lunchtime queues at the museum restaurant for bargain hot and cold dishes. There's an excellent choice of salads for vegetarians. Similar food is offered in the basement of the Gulbenkian museum, with outdoor seats facing the gardens.

CERVEJARIA TRINDADE

Centro de Lazer de Campo Pequeno 601 ☎ 217 964 000. Daily noon–11pm. MAP P.96–97, POCKET MAP J1

This branch of the historic beerhall (see p.67) is set within the outer ring of the bullring, with outdoor seats on the square. There are *bacalhau* dishes, steaks and octopus on offer. Mains from €9.

ELEVEN

Rua Marquês da Fronteira ☎ 213 862 211, ⓦ www.restauranteleven.com. Mon–Sat 12.30–3pm & 7.30–11pm. MAP P.96–97, POCKET MAP G4

At the top of Parque Eduardo VII, this Michelin-starred restaurant, under the watchful eye of German head chef Joachim Koerper, hits the heights both literally and metaphorically. The interior is both intimate and bright with wonderful city views. The food is expensive but not

ELEVEN

outrageous, with set menus from around €75 or a tasting menu at around €90. Dishes include black pork with chestnut gnocchi, veal with lemongrass and pumpkin risotto with scallops, and there's a fine wine list.

FRANGO DA GUIA

Campo Pequeno ☎ 217 961 031. Daily noon–11.30pm. MAP P.97, POCKET MAP J1.

This restaurant takes its inspiration from the Algarve village of Guia, which is famed for its spit-roast chicken. The version served here is a steal at €6. You'll also find steaks and other grills for around €8. Sit outside in the lovely space within the bullring's outer walls.

JARDIM DO SENTIDOS

Rua Mãe d'Água 3 ☎ 213 423 670. Mon–Fri noon–3pm & 7–10.30pm, Sat 7–10.30pm. MAP P.96–97, POCKET MAP J5

This attractive, long space opens onto a pleasant garden. The food is vegetarian, with set buffets featuring the likes of *tofu á bras* and decent lasagne.

MARISQUEIRA SANTA MARTA

Trav. do Enviato de Inglaterra 1 (off Rua de Santa Marta) ☎ 213 525 638. Daily noon–midnight. MAP P.96–97, POCKET MAP J4

Attractive and spacious *marisqueira* with bubbling tanks of crabs in one corner. Service is very attentive and meals end with a complimentary port, after which you don't usually care that the bill is slightly above average (mains from €12).

RIBADOURO

Avda da Liberdade 155 ☎ 213 549 411. Daily noon–1am. MAP P.96–97, POCKET MAP J5

The *avenida's* best *cervejaria*, serving superb mixed grills (around €13), speciality prawns with garlic (around €15) and pricier shellfish (but no fish). If you don't fancy a full meal, take a seat at the bar and order a beer with a plate of prawns. It's best to book for the restaurant, especially at weekends.

SALDANHA MAR

Rua Eng. Viera da Silva 2E ☎ 210 410 620. Daily 12.30–3pm & 7.30–11pm. MAP P.96–97, POCKET MAP J3

Chic, minimalist restaurant attached to the cool *Fontana Park* hotel (see p.134). Most of the sumptuous fish and seafood is shipped straight from the market opposite, combined with fresh seasonal produce; dishes such as sea bass with sautéed vegetables and filling fish stews start at around €15.

SOLAR DO MORAIS

Rua Augusto dos Santos 3 ☎ 213 143 840. Mon–Fri 9.30am–10.30pm. MAP P.96–97, POCKET MAP H3

A popular lunchtime spot for locals, despite its position between the tourist draws of Parque Eduardo VII and the Gulbenkian. The cool, arched interior has cabinets of fresh

A LINHA D'ÁGUA

food, bottles lining the walls and a large ham on the bar. Good-value trout and salmon dishes are always worth ordering, and there's a small outdoor terrace.

Cafés and bars

A LINHA D'ÁGUA

Jardim Amália Rodrigues ☎ 213 814 327. Daily 10am–8pm. MAP P.96–97, POCKET MAP G3

Facing a small lake, this glass-fronted café is at the northern end of the park. It's a tranquil spot to sip a coffee or beer, and decent buffet lunches are served too.

BELA IPANEMA

Avda da Liberdade 169 ☎ 213 572 316. Mon–Sat 7am–midnight. MAP P.96–97, POCKET MAP J5

A bustling café/bar/restaurant by the São Jorge cinema where a steady stream of locals pops in for pastries, light lunches, beers and coffees at the bar, or in its small dining area that serves very good-value food; outdoor tables face the avenue.

BOTEQUIM DO REI

Alameda Cardeal Cerejeira ☎ 213 160 891.
Tues–Sun 10am–10pm. MAP P.96–97, POCKET MAP H3

Fairly average food (meat/fish dishes) but the outdoor seating, right in the park by a small lake, is particularly tranquil, making this a good place to head for lunch or a drink. Take care here, though, after dark.

BOULEVARD CAFÉ

Avda Praia da Vitória 35a. Mon–Sat
7am–2am. MAP P.96–97, POCKET MAP J3

One of the few lively café-bars in these parts, a bright, modern space attracting a young crowd for coffees and cakes by day and drinks or decent-value meals in the evening, when the music drowns out the TV sets in the corners.

GALETO

Avda da República 14 ☎ 213 560 269. Daily
7am–3am. MAP P.96–97, POCKET MAP J2

Late-opening café/bar/restaurant with striking 1960s decor: dark, metal-studded walls and padded bar seats. There's a great range of snacks, pastries, beers and coffees, or you can perch at the bar for a full meal at sensible prices.

PANORAMA BAR

Sheraton Lisboa, Rua Latino Coelho 1 ☎ 213 120 000. Mon–Fri 12.30pm–2am, Sat & Sun 6pm–2am. MAP P.96–97, POCKET MAP J3

Stroll into this high-rise hotel and take the lift to the spectacular top-floor bar (open to the public). As you'd expect, drinks aren't cheap, but dubbed Lisbon's eighth hill, the bar commands the best views of the city you'll find outside of a plane.

PASTELARIA SANTA MARTA

Rua Rodrigues Sampaio 52 ☎ 213 533 901.
Mon–Sat 7am–8pm. MAP P.96–97, POCKET MAP J5

Unglamorous but popular local haunt with a superb array of cakes and snacks. A good spot for inexpensive breakfasts and lunches. Pay at the till on exit.

VERSAILLES

Avda da República 15a ☎ 213 546 340. Daily
7.30am–10pm. MAP P.96–97, POCKET MAP J2

Traditional café full of bustling waiters circling the starched tablecloths. It's busiest at around 4pm, when Lisbon's elderly dames gather for a chat beneath the chandeliers.

Live music

HOT CLUBE DE PORTUGAL

Praça da Alegria 39 ☎ 213 467 369, Ⓦ www
.hcp.pt. Tues–Sat 10pm–2am. MAP P.96–97,
POCKET MAP J5

Dating from 1948 – making it one of Europe's oldest jazz clubs – this tiny basement club hosts top names in the jazz world, along with a range of local performers. The current venue was largely rebuilt after a recent fire.

VERSAILLES

Parque das Nações

The Parque das Nações or "Park of Nations" (pronounced "na-soysh") is the high-tech former site of Expo 98. Its flat, pedestrianized walkways lined with fountains and futuristic buildings are in complete contrast to the narrow, precipitous streets of old Lisbon, and it is packed with locals on summer weekends. The main highlight is the giant Oceanário de Lisboa, but it also features a casino, a cable car, riverside walk- and cycle-ways, a giant park and two of Lisbon's largest concert venues. It is also impossible to miss the astonishing 17km-long Vasco da Gama bridge over the Tejo. Constructed in time for the Expo in 1998, it is still the longest bridge in Europe.

OLIVAIS DOCK AND THE PAVILHÃO ATLÂNTICO

MAP P.107, POCKET MAP B17-18

The central focus of the Parque das Nações is the Olivais dock, overlooked by pixie-hatted twin towers, and where boats pull in on Tejo cruises (see p.142). The dock's **Nautical Centre** (☎218 949 066) offers canoeing, sailing and windsurfing lessons. The main building facing the dock is the Pavilhão de Portugal (Portugal Pavilion), a multipurpose arena designed by Álvaro Siza Vieira, architect of the reconstructed Chiado district, featuring an enormous, sagging concrete canopy on its south side. Opposite here – past Antony Gormley's weird Rhizone sculpture, a tree of cast-iron legs – is the spaceship-like **Pavilhão Atlântico** (Atlantic Pavilion; ☎218 918 440, ⓦwww.pavilhaoatlantico .pt), Portugal's largest indoor arena and the venue for major visiting bands and sporting events. The MTV music awards were held here in 2005.

Visiting the park

The best way to reach the park is to take the metro to Oriente or bus #28 from Praça do Comércio. Oriente metro station exits in the bowels of the Estação do Oriente, a cavernous glass and concrete station designed by Spanish architect Santiago Calatrava.

The park's Posto de Informação (information desk; daily 10am–8pm, until 7pm from Oct–April; ☎218 919 333, ⓦwww.portaldasnacoes.pt) has details of the day's events.

It's easy to walk round the park, or there's a toy train, which trundles anticlockwise around the main sights (hourly 10am–7pm Sat & Sun only; until 5pm from Oct–April; €4). You can also hire bikes from Tejo Bike (daily 10am–7.30pm; Sat & Sun only until 6pm from April–Oct, ⓦwww.tejobike.pt) behind the information desk for €5 an hour which is long enough to cycle out along the riverfront to the Vaso de Gama bridge.

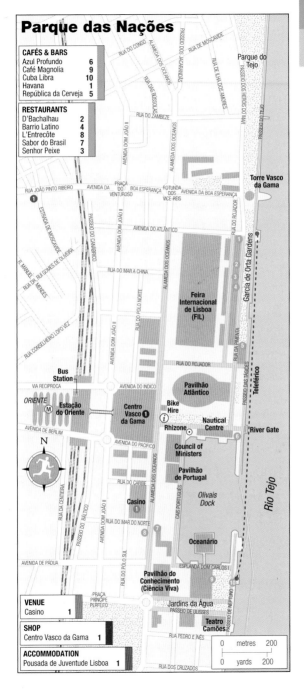

Parque das Nações

CAFÉS & BARS
Azul Profundo	6
Café Magnolia	9
Cuba Libra	10
Havana	1
República da Cerveja	5

RESTAURANTS
D'Bachalhau	2
Barrio Latino	4
L'Entrecôte	8
Sabor do Brasil	7
Senhor Peixe	3

VENUE
Casino	1

SHOP
Centro Vasco da Gama	1

ACCOMMODATION
Pousada de Juventude Lisboa	1

PAVILHÃO DO CONHECIMENTO (CIÊNCIA VIVA)

Alameda dos Oceanos ☎ 218 917 100.
ⓦ www.pavconhecimento.pt. Tues–Fri
10am–6pm, Sat & Sun 11am–7pm. €7,
children under 17 €4. MAP P.107, POCKET MAP B18

Run by Portugal's Ministry
of Science and Technology,
the Knowledge Pavilion
(Live Science) hosts excellent changing exhibitions on
subjects like 3D animation and
the latest computer technology,
and is usually bustling with
school parties. The permanent
interactive exhibits – allowing
you to create a vortex in water
or a film of detergent the size of
a baby's blanket – are particularly good and there's also a
cybercafé offering free internet.

JARDINS DA ÁGUA

MAP P.107, POCKET MAP B19

The Jardins da Água (Water
Gardens), crisscrossed by
waterways and ponds, are
based on the stages of a river's
drainage pattern, from stream
to estuary. They are not huge,
but linked by stepping stones,
and there are enough gushing
fountains, water gadgets

FOUNTAIN IN CAMINHO DA ÁGUA

and pumps to keep children
occupied for hours.

OCEANÁRIO

Esplanada Dom Carlos I ☎ 218 917 002.
ⓦ www.oceanario.pt. Daily May–Sept
10am–8pm, Oct–April 10am–7pm. €13,
children under 12 €6, family ticket €34. MAP
P.107, POCKET MAP B18

Designed by Peter Chermaeff
and looking like something off
the set of a James Bond film,
Lisbon's Oceanário (Oceanarium), is one of Europe's
largest and contains some 8,000
fish and marine animals. Its
main feature is the enormous
central tank which you can
look into from different levels
for close-up views of circling
sharks down to the rays
burying themselves into the
sand. Almost more impressive,
though, are the re-creations
of various ocean ecosystems,
such as the Antarctic tank,
containing frolicking penguins,
and the Pacific tank, where
otters bob about in the rock
pools. On a darkened lower
level, smaller tanks contain
shoals of brightly coloured
tropical fish and other warm-
water creatures. Find a window
free of school parties and the
whole experience becomes the
closest you'll get to deep-sea
diving without getting wet.

THE TELEFÉRICO AND THE JARDINS GARCIA DA ORTA

Mid-June to mid-Sept Mon–Fri 11am–8pm,
Sat & Sun 10am–8pm; Mid-Sept to mid-June
daily 10am–7pm. €4 one-way, €6.20 return.
Children under 14 €2 single, €3.50 return. MAP
P.107, POCKET MAP B16–18

The ski-lift-style *teleférico*
(cable car) rises up to 20m as it
shuttles you over Olivais Docks
to the northern side of the
Parque, giving commanding
views over the site on the way.
It drops down to the Garcia da
Orta gardens, containing exotic

trees from Portugal's former colonies. Behind the gardens, Rua Pimenta is lined with a motley collection of international restaurants, from Irish to Israeli.

TORRE VASCO DA GAMA

MAP P.107, POCKET MAP B16

Once an integral part of an oil refinery, the Torre Vasco da Gama (Vasco da Gama Tower) is, at 145m high, Lisbon's tallest structure. The tower is now integrated into a five-star hotel.

PARQUE DO TEJO

MAP P.107, POCKET MAP B15

Spreading along the waterfront for 2km right up to the Vasco da Gama bridge, Parque do Tejo is Lisbon's newest park, with bike trails and riverside walks. It's a great spot for a picnic – supplies are available from the supermarkets in the Vasco da Gama shopping centre and bike hire from Tejo Bike (see p.106).

FEIRA INTERNACIONAL DE LISBOA

🕾 218 921 500, 🖳 www.fil.pt. MAP P.107, POCKET MAP B16-17

Lisbon's trade fair hall, the Feira Internacional de Lisboa (FIL), hosts various events, including a handicrafts fair displaying ceramics and crafts from around the country (usually in July).

Vasco da Gama

The opening of Parque das Nações in 1998 celebrated the 500th anniversary of Vasco da Gama's arrival in India. One of Portugal's greatest explorers, Da Gama was born in Sines in 1460. By the 1490s he was working for João II protecting trading stations along the African coast. This persuaded the next king, Manuel I, to commission him to find a sea route to India. He departed Lisbon in July 1497 with a fleet of four ships, reaching southern Africa in December. The following May they finally reached Calicut in southwest India, obtaining trading terms before departing in August, 1498. The return voyage took a full year, by which time Da Gama had lost two of his ships and half his men. But he was richly rewarded by the king, his voyage inspiring Camões to write *Os Lusiadas*, Portugal's most famous epic poem. Da Gama returned to India twice more, the final time in 1524 when he contracted malaria and died in the town of Cochin.

CENTRO VASCO DA GAMA

Shops

CENTRO VASCO DA GAMA

Avda D. João II ☎ 218 930 601, 🌐 www
.centrovascodagama.pt. Daily 9am–midnight
MAP P.107, POCKET MAP A17

Three floors of local and
international stores are housed
under a glass roof, washed
by permanently running
water; international branches
include Zara, Timberland and
C&A and local sports and
bookshops also feature. There
are plenty of fast-food outlets
and good-value restaurants
on the top floor, ten cinema
screens, children's areas and a
huge Continente supermarket
on the lower floor.

Restaurants

BARRIO LATINO

Rua de Pimenta 31 ☎ 934 971 585, 🌐 www
.barriolatinolisboa.com. Daily noon–3am. MAP
P.107, POCKET MAP B16.

A decent bar and restaurant
(steak and fish from around

€12) but best known for its
riotous Afro-Latin dance
nights; from Wed to Sun there
are dance lessons, or just come
along and join in the fun.

D'BACALHAU

Rua do Pimenta 43–45 ☎ 218 941 297.
Mon–Sat noon–11.30pm, Sun noon–3pm. MAP
P.107, POCKET MAP B16.

If you want to sample one of
the alleged 365 recipes for
bacalhau – salted cod – this is a
good place to come, as it serves
quite a range of them from €9:
bacalhau com natas (with a
creamy sauce) is always good.
There are also other dishes,
including a selection of fresh
fish from €12.

L'ENTRECÔTE

Alameda dos Oceanos 10212a ☎ 218 962
220. Daily 12.30–3pm & 7.30–11.30pm. MAP
P.107, POCKET MAP B18

Local branch of the Lisbon
restaurant famed for its
fabulous steaks cooked with
sublime sauces – choose from
various menus starting at €8.

SABOR DO BRASIL

Alameda dos Oceanos 1990 ☎ 218 955 143.
Daily noon–3.30am & 7.30–11.30pm. MAP P.107,
POCKET MAP B18

This large space has outdoor
seats in a great position facing
the waters. Its name means
"taste of Brazil" and you can
sample a range of piquant
dishes such as spicy *moqueca*
fish, tropical salmon, *feijoada*
bean stews or *picanha* garlic
beef from €12–15.

SENHOR PEIXE

Rua da Pimenta 35–37 ☎ 218 955 892.
Tues–Sat noon–3am & 7.30–11pm, Sun
noon–3pm. MAP P.107, POCKET MAP B16.

"Mr Fish" is widely thought to
serve up some of the best fresh
seafood in the Lisbon region –
check the counter for the day's
catch or choose a lobster from

the bubbling tank. Most dishes – from around €15 – are grilled in the open kitchen. There's also a little fish-themed bar and pleasant outdoor tables.

Cafés and bars

AZUL PROFUNDO

Doca da Olivais. Daily 10am–2am, closes 10pm from Oct–April. MAP P.107, POCKET MAP B17

Sunny esplanade bar overlooking the glittering docks. Offers a good range of snacks, fruit juices and fantastic *caipirinha* cocktails along with inexpensive lunches.

CAFÉ MAGNOLIA

Esplanada Dom Carols 29 ☎ 218 968 214. Daily 10am–8pm (closes 6pm from Oct–April). MAP P.107, POCKET MAP B18

Adjoined to but independent of the Oceanarium, this bright little café has a counter stuffed with excellent pastries. It also does inexpensive toasts and filled crepes, with outdoor seating facing a pleasant lawned area and the river.

COFFEE AND PASTEL DE NATA

CUBA LIBRA

Passeio de Neptuno. Daily noon–4am, closes 6pm from Oct–April. MAP P.107, POCKET MAP B18

Breezy kiosk café-bar right by the river and under the cable-car run. It comes into its own on a warm evening when the *caipirinha* cocktails and rum punches lubricate proceedings.

HAVANA

Rua da Pimenta 115–117. Daily noon–2am, Sat & Sun only Oct–April. MAP P.107, POCKET MAP B16

Lively Cuban bar with an airy interior and outdoor seating. The pulsating Latin sounds get progressively louder after 11pm, when it turns into more of a club until 2am.

REPÚBLICA DA CERVEJA

Passeio das Tágides 2–26 ☎ 218 922 590. Daily 12.30pm–1am, closes midnight from Oct–Feb. MAP P.107, POCKET MAP B17

In a great position close to the water's edge and facing the Vasco da Gama bridge, this modern bar-restaurant specializes in some fine international beers, though sticking to the local Superbock will save a few euros. Steaks, burgers and sausages are also on offer (mains from €8–14), and there's live music Thurs–Sat.

Live music

CASINO

Alameda dos Oceanos ☎ 218 929 000, ⓦ www.casinolisboa.pt. Sun–Thurs 3pm–3am, Fri–Sat 4pm–4am. MAP P.107, POCKET MAP A18

Opened in 2006, this state-of-the-art space – with its glass cylinder entrance hall – hosts top shows from Broadway and London as well as major concerts in the performance hall, which has a retractable roof. The usual casino attractions also feature.

Sintra

If you make just one day-trip from Lisbon, choose the beautiful hilltop town of Sintra, the former summer residence of Portuguese royalty and a UNESCO World Heritage Site since 1995. Not only does the town boast two of Portugal's most extraordinary palaces, it also contains a semitropical garden, a Moorish castle, a top modern-art museum and proximity to some great beaches. Looping around a series of wooded ravines and with a climate that encourages moss and ferns to grow from every nook and cranny, Sintra consists of three districts: Sintra-Vila, with most of the historical attractions; Estefânia, a ten-minute walk to the east, where trains from Lisbon pull in; and São Pedro to the south, well known for its antique shops and best visited on the eve of São Pedro (June 28–29), the main saint's day, and for its market on the second and fourth Sunday of the month.

SINTRA-VILA

The historic centre of Sintra spreads across the slopes of several steep hills, themselves loomed over by wooded heights topped by the Moorish castle and the Palácio da Pena. Dominating the centre of Sintra-Vila are the tapering chimneys of the Palácio Nacional, surrounded by an array of tall houses painted in pale pink, ochre or mellow yellow, many with ornate turrets and decorative balconies peering out to the plains of Lisbon far below. All this is highly scenic – though in fact Sintra looks at its best seen on the way in from the station. Summer crowds can swamp the narrow central streets, and once you've seen the sights, you're best off heading to the surrounding attractions up in the hills.

Visiting Sintra

Sintra is served by regular trains from Lisbon's Rossio, Entre Campos and Sete Rios station (every 15–20min; 45min; €2 single). A land train (every 30min from 10.30am–dusk; €5 day ticket) runs from Sintra station to São Pedro and back via Sintra-Vila. Alternatively, bus #434 takes a circular route from Sintra station to most of the sites mentioned in this chapter (every 20min from 9.45am–6.15pm; €5) and allows you to get on and off whenever you like on the circuit. Also useful is bus #435 which runs from Sintra station to Monserrate gardens via Sintra-Vila and Quinta da Regaleira (every 30min 9.45am–6.45pm; €2) To see the area around Sintra, including the coast, consider a Day-rover (Turístico Diário) ticket on the local Scotturb buses (www.scotturb.com; €10). Ask at the tourist office about various combined tickets that can save money on entry to the main sites.

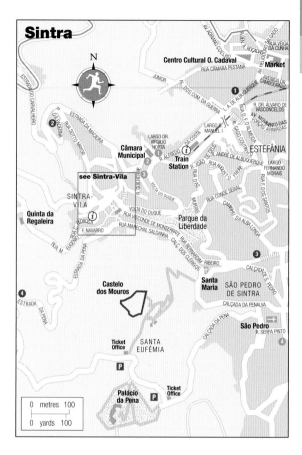

Sintra

Centro Cultural O. Cadaval

Market

Câmara Municipal

Train Station

ESTEFÂNIA

SINTRA-VILA

see Sintra-Vila

Quinta da Regaleira

Parque da Liberdade

Castelo dos Mouros

Santa Maria

SÃO PEDRO DE SINTRA

São Pedro

Ticket Office

SANTA EUFÉMIA

Palácio da Pena

Ticket Office

0 metres 100

0 yards 100

Sintra-Vila

Palácio Nacional

LARGO RAINHA D. AMÉLIA

PRAÇA DA REPÚBLICA

Museu do Brinquedo

LARGO FERREIRA DE CASTRO

ACCOMMODATION	
Casa da Valle	2
Chalet Relogio	4
Hotel Nova Sintra	1
Hotel Sintra Jardim	3

RESTAURANTS	
Cantinho de São Pedro	4
Páteo do Garrett	10
Restaurante Regional	1
A Tasca do Manel	2
Tulhas	8
CAFÉS	
Adega das Caves	6
Café Paris	5
Casa Piriquita	7
Fábrica das Verdadeiras Queijadas da Sapa	3
BAR & CLUB	
Bar Fonte da Pipa	9

PALÁCIO NACIONAL

Largo da Rainha Dona Amélia ☎ 219 106 840 ⓦ www.pnsintra.imc-ip.pt. Mon, Tues & Thurs–Sun 9.30am–6.30pm, closes 5.30pm from Oct–May. €7, free Sun 10am–2pm. MAP P.113

Best seen early or late in the day to avoid the crowds, the sumptuous Palácio Nacional was probably already in existence at the time of the Moors. It takes its present form from the rebuilding of Dom João I (1385–1433) and his successor, Dom Manuel I, the chief royal beneficiary of Vasco da Gama's explorations. Its exterior style is an amalgam of Gothic – featuring impressive battlements – and Manueline, tempered inside by a good deal of Moorish influences. Sadly, after the fall of the monarchy in 1910, most of the surrounding walls and medieval houses were destroyed. Highlights on the lower floor include the Manueline **Sala dos Cisnes**, so-called for the swans (*cisnes*) on its ceiling, and the Sala das Pegas, which takes its name from the flock of magpies (*pegas*) painted on the frieze and ceiling – João I, caught in the act of kissing a lady-in-waiting by his queen, reputedly

had the room decorated with as many magpies as there were women at court, to imply they were all magpie-like gossips.

Best of the upper floor is the gallery above the palace chapel. Beyond, a succession of **state rooms** finishes with the Sala das Brasões, its domed and coffered ceiling emblazoned with the arms of 72 noble families. Finally, don't miss the kitchens, whose roofs taper into the giant chimneys that are the palace's distinguishing features. The Palace also hosts events for the Sintra Music Festival (see p.146).

MUSEU DO BRINQUEDO

Rua Visconde de Monserrate 29 ☎ 219 242 171, ⓦ www.museu-do-brinquedo.pt. Tues–Sun 10am–6pm. €4, children under 12 €2. MAP P.113

Housed in a former fire station, the Museu do Brinquedo – a fascinating private toy collection – is a great place for children. The huge array of toys exhibited over three floors is somewhat confusingly labelled, but look out for the 3000-year-old stone Egyptian toys on the first floor, the 1930s Hornby trains and some of the first-ever toy cars, produced in Germany in the early 1900s. There are numerous cases of soldiers, early Portuguese toys including a selection of 1930s beach games, wooden toys from Senegal, wire bicycles from Zimbabwe, and a top floor stuffed with dolls and doll's house furniture. There's also a café and a small play area for young children.

QUINTA DA REGALEIRA

Daily: Feb–March & Oct 10am–6.30pm; April–Sept 10am–8pm; Nov–Jan 10am–5.30pm. Tours (90min) every 30min–60min; advance booking essential on ☏ 219 106 650; €10. Unguided visits €6. MAP P.113

The Quinta da Regaleira is one of Sintra's most elaborate estates. It was designed at the end of the nineteenth century by Italian architect and theatre set designer Luigi Manini for wealthy Brazilian merchant António Augusto Carvalho Monteiro. Manini's penchant for the dramatic is obvious: the principal building, the mock-Manueline Palácio dos Milhões, sprouts turrets and towers while the interior boasts Art Nouveau tiles and elaborate Rococo wooden ceilings.

The surrounding **gardens** shelter fountains, terraces and grottoes, with the highlight being the Initiation Well, inspired by the initiation practices of the Freemasons. Entering via a Harry Potter-esque revolving stone door, you walk down a moss-covered spiral staircase to the foot of the well and through a tunnel, which eventually resurfaces at the edge of a lake (though in winter you exit from a shorter tunnel so as not to disturb a colony of hibernating bats).

In summer, the gardens host occasional performances of live music, usually classical or jazz.

CASTELO DOS MOUROS

☏ 219 237 300, ⓦ www.parquedesintra.pt. Daily: April–mid Oct 9.30am–8pm; mid-Oct–March 10am–6pm. €6. MAP P.113

Reached on bus #434, or a steep drive, the ruined ramparts of the Castelo dos Mouros are truly spectacular. Built in the ninth century, the Moorish castle spans two rocky pinnacles, with the remains of a mosque spread midway between, and extraordinary views all around. Conquered in 1147 by Afonso Henriques, with the aid of Scandinavian Crusaders, the castle walls fell into disrepair over subsequent centuries, before Ferdinand II had them restored in the mid-nineteenth century.

If walking from Sintra, take Calçada dos Clérigos, near the church of Santa Maria. From here, a stone pathway leads all the way up to the lower slopes, where you can see a Moorish grain silo and a ruined twelfth-century church. To enter the castle itself, you'll need to walk further along the path to buy a ticket from the road exit and double back to the castle.

CASTELO DOS MOUROS

PALÁCIO DA PENA

PALÁCIO DA PENA

Estrada da Pena ☎ 219 237 300, ⓦ www
.parquedesintra.pt. Daily: April–Sept
9.45am–7pm; Oct–March 10am–6pm; last
entry 1hr before closing. Palace and gardens
€12 (€9 from Oct to March), gardens only
€6. MAP P.113

Bus #434 stops opposite the
lower entrance to Parque da
Pena, a stretch of rambling
woodland with a scattering of
lakes and follies. At the top of
the park, about twenty minutes'
walk from the entrance or a
short ride on a shuttle bus (€3
return), looms the fabulous
Palácio da Pena, a wild
fantasy of domes, towers,
ramparts and walkways,
approached through mock-
Manueline gateways and a
drawbridge that does not draw.
A compelling riot of kitsch, the
palace was built in the 1840s to
the specifications of Ferdinand

of Saxe-Coburg-Gotha,
husband of Queen Maria II,
with the help of the German
architect, Baron Eschwege. The
interior is preserved exactly as
it was left by the royal family
when they fled Portugal in
1910. The result is fascinating:
rooms of stone decorated to
look like wood, statues of
turbaned Moors nonchalantly
holding electric chandeliers
– it's all here. Of an original
convent, founded in the early
sixteenth century to celebrate
the first sight of Vasco da
Gama's returning fleet, only a
beautiful, tiled chapel and
Manueline cloister have been
retained.

You can also look round the
mock-Alpine **Chalet Condessa
d'Edla**, built by Ferdinand in
the 1860s as a retreat for his
second wife.

MONSERRATE

Estrada da Monserrate ☎ 219 237 300,
Ⓦ www.parquedesintra.pt Daily: April–Sept
9.30am–8pm; Oct–March 10am–6pm. €6.
Guided tours to palace daily at 10am & 3pm,
€5 extra. MAP BELOW

The name most associated
with the fabulous gardens and
palace of Monserrate is that of
William Beckford, the wealthiest untitled Englishman of
his age, who rented the estate
from 1793 to 1799, having been
forced to flee Britain after he
was caught in a compromising
position with a sixteen-year-old
boy. Setting about improving
the place, he landscaped a
waterfall and even imported a
flock of sheep from his estate.

Half a century later, a second
immensely rich Englishman,
Sir Francis Cook, bought the
estate and imported the head
gardener from Kew to lay out
water plants, tropical ferns and

palms, and just about every
known conifer. For a time
Monserrate boasted the only
lawn in Iberia, and it remains
one of Europe's most richly
stocked gardens, with over a
thousand different species of
subtropical trees and plants.

From the entrance, paths
lead steeply down through
lush undergrowth to a ruined
chapel, half engulfed by a giant
banyan tree. From here, lawns
take you up to Cook's main
legacy, a great **Victorian palace**
inspired by Brighton Pavilion,
with its mix of Moorish and
Italian decoration – the dome
is modelled on the Duomo in
Florence. The interior has been
restored after years of neglect,
and you can now admire the
amazingly intricate plasterwork
which covers almost every wall
and ceiling. The park also has a
decent café (daily 10am–6pm).

AZENHAS DO MAR

Bus #441 from Sintra (every 1–2hr; 40min).
MAP P.117

Whitewashed cottages tumble down the steep cliff face at the pretty village of Azenhas do Mar, one of the most characterful villages of the Sintra coast. The beach is small, but there are artificial seawater pools for swimming in when the ocean is too rough.

PRAIA DAS MAÇÃS

Bus #441 from Sintra (every 1–2hr; 30min); or Praia das Maçãs tram from Sintra (see box opposite). MAP P.117

The largest and liveliest resort on this coast, Praia das Maçãs is also the easiest to reach from Sintra – take the tram (see box opposite) for the most enjoyable journey. Along with a big swath of sand, Praia das Maçãs has an array of bars and restaurants to suit all budgets.

PRAIA GRANDE

Bus #441 from Sintra (every 1–2hr; 25min).
MAP P.117

Set in a wide, sandy cliff-backed bay, this is one of the best and safest beaches on the Sintra coast, though its breakers attract surfers aplenty. In August the World Bodyboarding Championships are held here, along with games such as volleyball and beach rugby. Plenty of inexpensive cafés and restaurants are spread out along the beachside road, and if the sea gets too rough, there are giant sea pools on the approach to the beach (June–Sept, €10).

PRAIA DA ADRAGA

No public transport; by car, follow the signs from the village of Almoçageme.
MAP P.117

Praia da Adraga was flatteringly voted one of Europe's best beaches by a British newspaper; the unspoilt, cliff-backed, sandy bay with just one beach restaurant is certainly far quieter than the other resorts, but it takes the full brunt of the Atlantic, so you'll need to take great care when swimming.

Quaint old trams shuttle from near the Centro Cultural Olga Cadaval to the coastal resort of Praia das Maçãs via Colares (April–Sept Fri–Sun four daily, 45min. €2 single). However, check the latest routes and timetables on ☎ 219 233 919 or in the Sintra tourist office, as there are frequent shortenings of the route or alterations to the service.

CABO DA ROCA

Bus #403 from Sintra or Cascais train stations (every 90min; 45min). MAP P.117

Little more than a windswept rocky cape with a lighthouse, this is the most westerly point in mainland Europe, which guarantees a steady stream of visitors – get there early to avoid the coach parties. You can soak up the views from the café-restaurant and handicraft shop (daily 9.30am–7.30pm) and buy a certificate to prove you've been here at the little tourist office (daily 9am–8pm, closes 7pm from Oct–May ☏ 219 280 081).

CONVENTO DOS CAPUCHOS

☏ 219 237 381; daily: April–mid-Oct 9.30am–8pm; mid-Oct–March 10am–6pm. €6. No public transport. A return taxi from Sintra with a 1hr stopover costs around €30. MAP P.117

If you have your own transport, don't miss a trip to the Convento dos Capuchos, an extraordinary hermitage with tiny, dwarf-like cells cut from the rock and lined with cork – hence its popular name of the Cork Convent. It was occupied for three hundred years until being finally abandoned in 1834 by its seven remaining monks, who must have found the gloomy warren of rooms and corridors too much to maintain. Some rooms – the penitents' cells – can only be entered by crawling through 70cm-high doors; here, and on every other ceiling, doorframe and lintel, are attached panels of cork, taken from the surrounding woods. Elsewhere, you'll come across a washroom, kitchen, refectory, tiny chapels, and even a bread oven set apart from the main complex.

PENINHA

MAP P.117

With your own transport, it is worth exploring the dramatic wooded landscape between Capuchos and Coba da Roca, much of it studded with giant moss-covered boulders. Some 3km from Capuchos lies Peninha, a spectacularly sited hermitage perched on a granite crag. The sixteenth-century Baroque interior is usually locked, but climb up anyway to get dazzling views of the Sintra coast towards Cascais. You can also take a waymarked 4.5km trail round the crag; otherwise it is a short return walk from the woodland car park.

CONVENTO DOS CAPUCHOS

Restaurants

CANTINHO DE SÃO PEDRO

Praça D. Fernando II 18, São Pedro de
Sintra ☎ 219 230 267. Daily noon–3pm &
7.30–10pm. MAP P.113

Large restaurant with bare
stone walls overlooking an
attractive courtyard just off
São Pedro's main square.
Slightly formal service but
excellent food at reasonable
prices. On cool evenings a log
fire keeps things cosy.

COLARES VELHO

Largo Dr Carlos de Franca 1–4, Colares
☎ 219 292 727. Tues–Sat 10am–11pm, Sun
10am–8pm.

Delightful restaurant and
teahouse in the tiny main
square of Colares, on the
road between Sintra and the
beaches. Traditional Portuguese
cuisine, such as *bacalhau*, starts
at €15; alternatively, take a seat
for some fine tea and cakes.

O LOUREIRO

Rua Pedro A. Cabral 6, Praia das Maçãs
☎ 219 292 442. Mon–Wed & Fri–Sun
11am–3pm & 7–11pm.

In a prime location overlooking
the beach, this is the best
place to try good-value local
fresh fish and seafood; the
grilled squid is always a good

and inexpensive choice. The
café-bar of the same name
opposite is also a good spot for
inexpensive drinks.

PÁTEO DO GARRETT

Rua Maria Eugénia Reis F. Navarro 7 ☎ 219
243 380, ⊕ www.pateodogarrett.com. Mon,
Tues & Thurs–Sun 11am–11pm; Jan–April
11am–2pm.

Although this café-restaurant
has a dark, dim interior, it's
also got a lovely sunny patio
offering fine views over the
village. Serves pork and apple
sauce, monkfish rice and the
like from around €12, or just
pop in for a drink.

RESTAURANTE REGIONAL DE SINTRA

Travessa do Município 2 ☎ 219 234 444. Mon,
Tues & Thurs–Sun noon–4pm & 7–10.30pm.
MAP P.113.

In a lovely old building next
to the Câmara Municipal, this
traditional and slightly formal
restaurant serves reliably tasty
dishes at reasonable prices –
fresh fish from €10, grilled
meats from €9 and a very
good *crepe de marisco* (seafood
crepe) for €9.

A TASCA DO MANEL

Largo Dr. Virgílio Horta 5. ☎ 219 230 215.
Mon–Sat 10am–10pm. MAP P.113
In total contrast to Sintra's

QUEIJADAS DA SINTRA

CAFÉ PARIS

wonderfully ornate Town Hall opposite, this is a very simple little *tasca* with cured hams hanging over the bar. Squeeze into a table for very good-value, no-nonsense fish and grills from under €7.

TULHAS

Rua Gil Vicente 4 ☎219 232 378. Mon, Tues & Thurs–Sun noon–3.30pm & 7–10pm. MAP P.113

Imaginative cooking in a fine building converted from old grain silos – the old grain well takes pride of place in the floor. The giant mixed grills at €24 for two people will keep carnivores more than happy, while the weekend specials are usually excellent with meat and fish from around €9.

Cafés

ADEGA DAS CAVES

Rua da Pendoa 2. ☎ 219 239 848. Daily 9am–2am. MAP P.113

Bustling café-bar below *Café Paris* (see below) attracting a predominantly local and youthful clientele; the adjacent restaurant at no. 8 does meals from around €9.

CAFÉ PARIS

Largo Rainha D. Amélia ☎219 232 375. Daily 8am–midnight. MAP P.113

This attractive blue-tiled café is the highest-profile in town, which means steep prices for not especially exciting food, although it is a great place for a cocktail. Reservations are advised in high season.

CASA PIRIQUITA

Rua das Padarias 1 ☎219 230 626. Mon, Tues & Thurs–Sun 9am–midnight. MAP P.113

Cosy tearoom and bakery, which can get busy with locals queueing to buy *queijadas da Sintra* (sweet cheesecakes) and other pastries.

FÁBRICA DAS VERDADEIRAS QUEIJADAS DA SAPA

Volta do Duche 12 ☎219 230 493. Tues–Sun 9am–6pm & 7–9pm. MAP P.113

This old-fashioned café is famed for its traditional *queijadas*, made on the premises for over a century. It's a bit dingy inside, so it's best to buy takeaways to sustain you on your walk to the centre.

Bars and clubs

BAR FONTE DA PIPA

Rua Fonte da Pipa 11–13 ☎219 234 437. Daily 9pm–2am. MAP P.113

Laidback bar with low lighting and comfy chairs. It's up the hill from *Casa Piriquita*, next to the lovely ornate fountain (*fonte*) that the street is named after.

MAÇAS CLUB

Rua Pedro Álvaro Cabral 10, Praia das Maçãs ☎219 292 024, ⊕www.macasclub.com. Tues–Sun: 10am–2am, club Sat 11pm–4am.

Set just off the beach, this fashionable café/bar/club is the social hub of the village. Guest DJs feature at weekends.

The Lisbon coast

Lisbon's most accessible beaches lie along the Cascais coast just beyond the point where the Tejo flows into the Atlantic. Famed for its casino, Estoril has the best sands, though neighbouring Cascais has more buzz. The River Tejo separates Lisbon from high-rise Caparica, to the south, on a superb stretch of wave-pounded beach, popular with surfers.

ESTORIL

With its grandiose villas, luxury hotels and health spa, Estoril (pronounced é-stril) has pretensions towards being a Portuguese Riviera. The centre is focused on the leafy **Parque do Estoril** and its enormous casino (Tues–Sat 3pm–3am; free; semi-formal attire required ;☎ 214 667 700, ⓦ www.casino-estoril.pt). During World War II, this was where exiled royalty hung out and many spies made their names. Ian Fleming was based here to keep an eye on double agents, and used his experience at the casino as inspiration for the first James Bond novel *Casino Royale*.

The resort's fine sandy beach, **Praia de Tamariz**, is backed by some ornate villas and a seafront promenade that stretches northwest to Cascais,

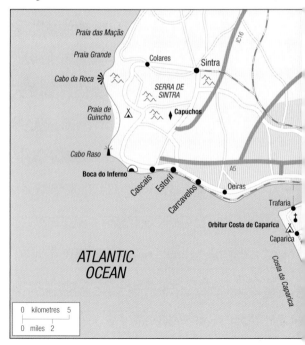

THE LISBON COAST

a pleasant twenty-minute stroll. In summer, firework displays take place above the beach every Saturday at midnight.

Estoril is also famed for its world-class **golf courses** which lie a short distance inland (info at ⓦwww.portugalgolf.com); it also hosts the Estoril Open tennis tournament in May (ⓦwww.estorilopen.net).

Transport to Estoril and Cascais

Trains from Lisbon's Cais do Sodré (every 20min; 35min to Estoril, 40min to Cascais; €2 single) wend along the shore. There are also regular buses to and from Sintra, or it's a fine drive down the corniche.

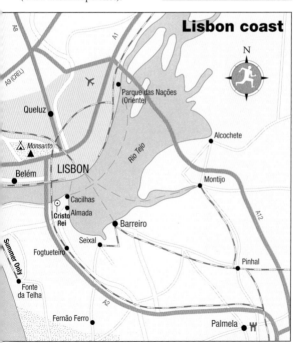

123

CASCAIS

MAP BELOW

Cascais (pronounced cash-kaysh) is a highly attractive former fishing village, liveliest round Largo Luis de Camões, at one end of Rua Frederico Arouca, the main mosaic-paved pedestrian thoroughfare. Nearby is the **fish market** (Mon–Fri), best in the afternoon after the catch comes in.

Praia da Conceição is the best beach to lounge on or try out watersports. The rock-fringed smaller beaches of **Praia da Rainha** and **Praia da Ribeira** are off the central stretch, while regular buses run 6km northwest to **Praia do Guincho**, a fabulous sweep of surf-beaten sands.

Cascais is at its most charming in the grid of streets north of the **Igreja da Assunção** – its azulejos predate the earthquake of 1755. Nearby, on Rua Júlio Pereiro de Melo, the engaging **Museu do Mar** (☎214 815 906; Tues–Sun 10am–5pm; free) relates the town's relationship with the sea, with model boats, treasure from local wrecks, fossils and stuffed fish.

CASA DAS HISTÓRIAS

Avda Da República 300 ☎214 826 970, 🌐 www.casadashistoriaspaularego.com Daily 10am–6pm. Free. MAP BELOW.

The distinctive ochre towers of the modernist **Casa das Histórias** mark a fantastic museum which, unusually, is dedicated to a living artist, Paula Rego. Designed by famous architect Eduardo Souto de Moura, the airy museum features over 120 of her disturbing but beautiful collages, pastels

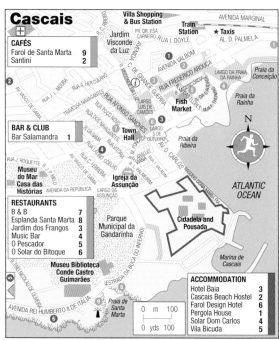

Cascais

CAFÉS
Farol de Santa Marta 9
Santini 2

BAR & CLUB
Bar Salamandra 1

RESTAURANTS
B & B 7
Esplanda Santa Marta 8
Jardim dos Frangos 3
Music Bar 4
O Pescador 5
O Solar do Bitoque 6

Villa Shopping & Bus Station
Train Station
★ Taxis
AVENIDA MARGINAL
AL. D. PALMELA

Jardim Visconde da Luz

Fish Market

Town Hall

Museu do Mar
Casa das Histórias

Igreja da Assunção

Parque Municipal da Gandarinha

Cidadela and Pousada

Museu Biblioteca Conde Castro Guimarães

Praia de Santa Marta

ATLANTIC OCEAN

Marina de Cascais

ACCOMMODATION
Hotel Baia 3
Cascais Beach Hostel 6
Farol Design Hotel 2
Pergola House 1
Solar Dom Carlos 4
Vila Bicuda 5

0 m 100
0 yds 100

and engravings as well as those by her late English husband Victor Willing. Many of her works explore themes of power: women and animals are portrayed as both powerful and sexually vulnerable; men often appear as fish or dressed in women's clothes.

AROUND CASCAIS MARINA

MAP OPPOSITE

The leafy **Parque Municipal da Gandarinha**, complete with picnic tables and playground, makes a welcome escape from the beach crowds. In one corner stands the mansion of the nineteenth-century Count of Guimarães, preserved complete with its fittings as the **Museu Biblioteca Conde Castro Guimarães** (📞214 815 304, 🌐www.cm-cascais.pt; Tues–Sun 10am–5pm; closes 1–2pm on Sat and Sun; free). Its most valuable exhibits are rare illuminated sixteenth-century manuscripts.

To the east, the walls of Cascais' largely seventeenth-century fortress (now partly a *pousada* hotel) guard the entrance to the **Marina de Cascais**, an enclave of expensive yachts serviced by restaurants, bars and boutiques.

CAPARICA

Via Rapida express (hourly; 30min) or slower local buses (every 15–30min; 50min), from Cacilhas or from Lisbon's Areeiro/Praça de Espanha (every 30–60min; 40–60min).

According to legend, Caparica was named after the discovery of a cloak (*capa*) full of golden coins. Today it is a slightly tacky, high-rise seaside resort, but don't let that put you off: it's family friendly, has plenty of good seafood as well as several kilometres of soft sandy beach popular with surfers.

From June to October, buses stop right near the sands – at other times get off at the first stop in Caparica, on the edge of the tree-lined Praça da Liberdade, five minutes from the beach. From here, the pedestrianized Rua dos Pescadores heads down to the seafront.

From the beach, a **narrow-gauge mini-railway** (May–Sept daily every 30min from 9am–7.30pm; €6.50 return, or €4.50 return for first nine stops) runs south along the beach for 8km to the smaller resort of **Fonte da Telha**. You can jump off at any of the nineteen stops en route; earlier stops tend to be family-oriented, while later ones are younger, with nudity common.

Restaurants

O BARBAS

Rua Praia 13, Caparica ☎ 212 900 163. Mon, Tues & Thurs noon–2am.

Not quite the same since it moved into its two adjacent modern wood-framed buildings, *O Barbas* (*The Beard*) is nevertheless an atmospheric beach restaurant with affordable fish, *paella* and *cataplanas* to die for. You'll probably see the owner – he's the one with the huge amounts of facial hair.

B & B

Rua do Poço Novo 15, Cascais ☎ 214 820 686. Daily noon–10pm. MAP P.124

A small, intimate diner in the old town, specializing in tender steaks (around €12). Also does a few fresh fish dishes, omelettes and salads and great desserts – save room for the chocolate cake.

ESPLANADA SANTA MARTA

Avda Rei Humberto II de Italia, Cascais ☎ 214 837 779. Tues–Sat 10am–10pm. MAP P.124

One of the best places to

enjoy charcoal-grilled fish and savouries (from €8), which are served on a tiny terrace overlooking the sea and a little beach.

JARDIM DOS FRANGOS

Avda Com. Grande Guerra 68 ☎ 214 861 717, Cascais. Daily 10am–midnight. MAP P.124

Permanently buzzing with people and sizzling with the speciality, bargain grilled chicken from around €7, which is devoured by the plateful at indoor and outdoor tables. Get there early to guarantee a table as it is very popular.

MUSIC BAR

Largo Praia da Rainha 121, Cascais ☎ 214 820 848. June–Sept daily 10am–10pm; Oct–May closed Mon. MAP P.124

Great sea views are to be had inside or out on the raised terrace at this bustling café-restaurant. It's a fine spot to have a sunset beer. It also does decent, moderately priced fish, pasta and grilled meats (around €12).

O PESCADOR

Rua das Flores 10, Cascais ☎ 214 832 054, Mon–Sat noon–3.30pm & 6.30–11pm. MAP P.124

The best of a row of lively restaurants near the fish market, offering upmarket seafood – expect to pay over €25 for superb mains such as lobster baked in salt or tuna cooked in olive oil and garlic.

PRAIA DO TAMARIZ

Praia do Tamariz, Estoril ☎ 214 681 010. Daily April–Oct 9am–10pm, Nov–March noon–6pm.

High-profile restaurant right on the seafront promenade – which makes the fish, meat and pasta dishes pretty good value (mains cost from €10–15). Also a great spot for a sangria or *caipirinha*.

JONAS BAR, MONTE ESTORIL

SURFERS, CAPRICA BEACH

O SOLAR DO BITOQUE

Rua Regimento 19 de Infantaria Loja 11, Cascais ☎ 918 580 343. Mon–Sat 10am–midnight. MAP P.124

Bitoques are thin steaks, and this lively local with outdoor seating specializes in various types as well as burgers, salads and fresh fish. Very good value, with most dishes under €6.

Cafés

FAROL DE SANTA MARTA

Rua do Farol, Cascais. Tues–Sun: May–Sept 10am–7pm, Oct–April 10am–5pm. MAP P.124

Attached to a small lighthouse museum, this little café has an idyllic suntrap of a terrace, a perfect spot for a drink overlooking the sea.

SANTINI

Avenida Valbom 28F ☎ 214 833 709. Daily 11am–midnight. MAP P.124.

Opened by an Italian immigrant just after World War II, *Santini*'s delicious ice creams are legendary in these parts.

Bars and clubs

CHEQUERS

Largo Luís de Camões 7, Cascais ☎ 214 830 926. Daily: May–Sept 8am–2am, Oct–April 8am–8pm. MAP P.124

An English-style pub that fills up early with a good-time crowd; it serves so-so meals, too, and shows live soccer on TV, though most people come for drinks at tables outside in the attractive square.

JONAS BAR

Passeio Marítimo, Monte Estoril ☎ 214 676 946. Daily: May–Sept 8am–2am, Oct–April 8am–8pm. MAP P.124

Right on the seafront just north of Estoril, this is a laid-back spot day or night, selling cocktails, juices and snacks until the small hours.

BAR SALAMANDRA

Praia da Duquesa, Cascais ☎ 214 820 287. Daily noon–2am. MAP P.124

Some 200m from the station towards Estoril, with a great view of the seafront, *Salamandra* has something for everyone, from bar games to live TV sports and frequent live music. Also serves snacks.

TARQUINIO BAR

Muralha da Praia, Caparica ☎ 212 900 053, ⓦ www.tarquiniobar.com. Tues, Wed & Sun 10am–2am, Fri and Sat 9am–2am.

A popular surfers' hangout right on the seafront promenade, with full meals, snacks, drinks and cocktails – chill out on an array of chairs from deckchairs to bean bags and try the *caparica especial*, a fine mix of port and fresh orange.

ACCOMMODATION

Hotels and guesthouses

Lisbon's hotels range from sumptuous five stars to backstreet hideaways packed with local character. The grander ones tend to be found along Avenida da Liberdade, around Parque Eduardo VII or out of the centre. Better still, opt for one of the places in the Baixa, Alfama or round Bairro Alto. Besides hotels, there are pensions (*pensões*; singular *pensão*), guesthouses (*residenciais*; singular *residencial*) and various good-value hostels.

   Prices given are for a night in the cheapest double room in high season. Rates drop considerably out of season. Unless otherwise stated, all the places reviewed below have an en-suite bath or shower and include breakfast (anything from bread, jam and coffee to a generous spread of rolls, cereals, croissants, cold meat, cheese and fruit).

The Baixa and Rossio

HOTEL AVENIDA PALACE > Rua 1° de Dezembro 123 Ⓜ Restauradores ☎ 213 218 100, Ⓦ www.hotelavenidapalace .pt. MAP P.29, POCKET MAP C11 Built at the end of the nineteenth century, and rumoured to have a secret door direct to neighbouring Rossio station, this is one of Lisbon's grandest hotels. Despite extensive modernization, the traditional feel has been maintained with chandeliers and period furniture throughout. There are 82 spacious rooms, each with high ceilings and colossal bathrooms. €200

HOTEL DUAS NAÇÕES > Rua da Vitória 41 Ⓜ Rossio ☎ 213 460 710, Ⓦ www.duasnacoes.com. MAP P.29, POCKET MAP D12 Classy, pleasantly faded nineteenth-century hotel with helpful, English-speaking reception staff. Also has rooms for three to four people. €60; €30 extra for en-suite facilities

HOTEL EVIDENCIA TEJO > Rua dos Condes de Monsanto 2 Ⓜ Rossio ☎ 218 866 182, Ⓦ www.evidenciatejo .com. MAP P.29, POCKET MAP E11 This historic Baixa townhouse has been given a superb makeover, and now combines bare brickwork with cutting-edge design. Wood-floored rooms aren't huge but come with modems and minibars, and downstairs there is a boutiquey, Gaudi-inspired bar. €135

HOTEL METRÓPOLE > Rossio 30, Ⓜ Restauradores ☎ 213 219 030, Ⓦ www.almeidahotels.com. MAP P.29, POCKET MAP D11 Early twentieth century-era three-star, with an airy lounge bar offering superb views over Rossio and the castle. The simply furnished but spacious rooms are comfortable, but the square can be quite noisy at night. €185

HOTEL SUÍÇO ATLÂNTICO > Rua da Glória 9, Ⓜ Restauradores ☎ 213 461 713, Ⓦ www.turimhoteis .com. MAP P.29, POCKET MAP C10 In the last war, this was known to be the spies' favourite hangout – now it's a popular budget hotel in a good location, close to the *elevador* to Bairro Alto. Rooms are fairly standard, though some come with balconies looking down on to seedy Rua da Glória. €65

PENSÃO GERÊS > Calçada da Garcia 6 Ⓜ Rossio ☎ 218 810 497, Ⓦ www .pensaogeres.com. MAP P.29, POCKET MAP D10. Set on a steep side street

Booking a room

The main tourist offices (see p.131 for details) can provide accommodation lists, but won't reserve rooms for you. In the summer months, confirm a reservation at least a week in advance and get written confirmation; most owners understand English. Look out, too, for deals on hotel websites which are usually cheaper than walk-in rates.

just off Rossio, the beautiful, tiled entrance hall and chunky wooden doors set the tone for one of the more characterful central options. The simple rooms of varying sizes are minimally furnished, though all have TV and bathroom. Internet access on request; no breakfast. €55

PENSÃO PORTUENSE > Rua das Portas de Santo Antão 149–157 Ⓜ Restauradores ☎ 213 464 197, ⓦ www.pensaoportuense.com. MAP P.29, POCKET MAP J5. Singles, doubles and triples in a family-run guesthouse in a great position. Recently renovated, all rooms come with a/c and TVs and there's internet access. €65

RESIDENCIAL FLORESCENTE > Rua das Portas de Santo Antão 99 Ⓜ Restauradores ☎ 213 426 609, ⓦ www.residencialflorescente .com. MAP P.29, POCKET MAP J5 The best guesthouse on this pedestrianized street. There's a large selection of air-conditioned rooms across four floors (some en-suite with TV), so if you don't like the look of the room you're shown – and some are very cramped – ask about alternatives. Street-facing rooms can be noisy. There is also a lounge plus internet access for a small fee. €65

RESIDENCIAL INSULANA > Rua da Assunção 52 Ⓜ Rossio ☎ 213 427 625, ⓦ www.insulana.net. MAP P.29, POCKET MAP D12 Go upstairs past a series of shops to reach one of the more appealing Baixa options. With its own bar overlooking a quiet pedestrianized street, the hotel's smart rooms are complete with satellite TV and a/c. English-speaking staff. €65

VIP SUITES EDEN > Praça dos Restauradores 24 Ⓜ Restauradores ☎ 213 216 600, ⓦ www.viphotels.com. MAP P.29, POCKET MAP C10 Compact studios and apartments sleeping up to four people are available within the impressively converted Eden cinema. Get a ninth-floor apartment with a balcony and you'll have the best views and be just below the superb breakfast bar and rooftop pool. All come with dishwashers, microwaves and satellite TV. Disabled access. Studios from €100

The Sé, Castelo and Alfama

ALBERGARIA SENHORA DO MONTE > Calçada do Monte 39, Tram 28 ☎ 218 866 002, ⓦ www.albergariasenhorado monte.com. MAP P.40–41, POCKET MAP L5 Comfortable, modern hotel in a sublime location with views of the castle and Graça convent from the south-facing rooms, some of which have terraces. Breakfast is taken on the fourth-floor terrace, and private parking is available. Head north from Largo da Graça, taking the first left into Rua Damasceno Monteiro – Calçada do Monte is the first right. €90

PALACETE CHAFARIZ D'EL REI > Trav. Chafariz d'El Rei 6, Tram 25 ☎ 218 886 150, ⓦ www.chafarizdelrei.com. MAP P.40–41, POCKET MAP G12 Luxury guesthouse built in 1909 by a wealthy Brazilian merchant and lovingly restored a century later. From the reception – flooded with light from stained-glass windows – to the mirror room and library, the house is a stunning mix of Brazilian Art Nouveau and neo-Arabic flamboyance. Huge rooms, most with river views, have chandeliers and modern bathrooms while stonking breakfasts keep you going till dinner time. €200

131

PENSÃO NINHO DAS ÁGUIAS >
Costa do Castelo 74 , Tram 12 ☎ 218
854 070. MAP P.40–41, POCKET MAP
E11 Superbly sited in its own view-laden
terrace-garden just below the castle,
this is justifiably one of the most popular
budget places in the city. The 16 rooms
are spartan but bright, though avoid the
dingy basement room. Book in advance.
No breakfast. €45 for shared facilities,
otherwise €55

PENSÃO SÃO JOÃO DA PRAÇA >
Rua de São João da Praça 97–2° & 3°,
Tram 28 ☎ 218 862 591. MAP P.40–41,
POCKET MAP F12 Attractive townhouse
with street-facing wrought-iron balconies.
There's a range of rooms, the best on the
top floor with river views. From €35 with
shared bathroom, up to €55 with bath

SOLAR DO CASTELO > Rua das
Cozinhas 2, Bus 37 ☎ 218 806 050,
Ⓦ www.heritage.pt. MAP P.40–41,
POCKET MAP F11 A tastefully renovated
eighteenth-century mansion abutting the
castle walls on the site of the former
palace kitchens, parts of which remain.
Its 14 rooms cluster around a tranquil
inner courtyard, where you can enjoy a
vast buffet breakfast. It's not cheap and
rooms aren't enormous, but most boast
balconies overlooking the castle grounds,
and service is second to none. €200

SOLAR DOS MOUROS Rua do Milagre
de Santo António 6, Tram 28 ☎ 218 854
940, Ⓦ www.solardosmouros.com. MAP
P.40–41, POCKET MAP F12 A tall Alfama
townhouse done out in a contemporary
style with its own bar. Each of the twelve
rooms offers fantastic vistas of the river
(€25 extra) or castle and comes with CD
player and a/c. There's plenty of modern
art to enjoy if you tire of the view. €130;
breakfast €13 extra

Chiado and
Cais do Sodré

HOTEL BAIRRO ALTO > Praça Luís de
Camões 2 Ⓜ Baixa-Chiado. ☎ 213 408
223, Ⓦ www.bairroaltohotel.com.
MAP P.53, POCKET MAP C12 A grand
eighteenth-century building that has been
modernized into a fashionable boutique
hotel. Rooms and communal areas still
have a period feel – the lift takes a deep
breath before rattling up its six floors – but
modern touches appear in the form of DVDs
in rooms, a rooftop café and a swish
split-level bar full of comfy cushions. €250

HOTEL BORGES > Rua Garrett 108
Ⓜ Baixa-Chiado. ☎ 213 461 951,
Ⓦ www.lisbonhotelborges.com. MAP
P.53, POCKET MAP C12 In a prime spot
on Chiado's main street, this traditional
and elegantly furnished three-star is very
popular, though front rooms can be noisy.
Double or triple rooms are plain and
small but good value. €90

HOTEL DO CHIADO > Rua Nova do
Almada 114 Ⓜ Baixa-Chiado. ☎ 213
256 100, Ⓦ www.hoteldochiado.com.
MAP P.53, POCKET MAP D12 Designed by
architect Álvaro Siza Viera, this stylish
hotel has lovely communal areas –
orange segment-shaped windows give
glimpses of Chiado in one direction and
the whole city in the other. The cheapest
rooms lack much of an outlook, but the
best ones have terraces with stunning
views towards the castle – a view you get
from the bar terrace too. All rooms have
wi-fi. Limited parking available. €125

LX BOUTIQUE > Rua do Alecrim
12 Ⓜ Cais do Sodré ☎ 213 474 394,
Ⓦ www.lxboutiquehotel.pt. MAP P.53,
POCKET MAP C13. A tasteful makeover to
an old townhouse has made *LX Boutique*
into a popular small hotel with its own
chic restaurant. The *Boutique* refers to
its themed floors named after Portuguese
poets and fado singers. Rooms are all
stylish and individual, with shutters
and tasteful lighting – try and get one
with river views rather than over the
unsalubrious Rua Nova do Carvalho. €100

Bairro Alto and
São Bento

CASA DE SÃO MAMEDE > Rua da
Escola Politécnica 159, Bus 1 ☎ 213
963 166, Ⓦ www.casadesaomamede
.com. MAP P.62–63, POCKET MAP H5 On
a busy street north of Príncipe Real, this

Author picks

BUDGET *Lisbon Lounge Hostel* p.137
DESIGNER *Inspira* p.134
RETRO CHIC *Heritage Avenida* p.134
FAMILY *Vila Bicuda* p.136
HISTORIC *Palacete Chafariz d'el Rei* p.131

is a superb eighteenth-century former magistrate's house with period fittings, bright breakfast room and a grand stained-glass window. Rooms are rather ordinary, but all are equipped with a TV and a/c. **€90**

HOTEL ANJO AZUL > Rua Luz Soriano 75, Bus 1 🚊 213 478 069, 🌐 www .blueangelhotel.com. MAP P.62–63, POCKET MAP B11 The "Blue Angel" is best known for being gay friendly, but is not exclusively so. Set in a lovely blue-tiled townhouse right in the heart of the area's nightlife, there are 20 simple but attractive rooms set over four floors (€50), some with en-suite facilities (€65). No breakfast; however, there is a communal kitchen. **From €50**

HOTEL PRINCÍPE REAL > Rua da Alegria 53, Bus 1 🚊 213 407 350, 🌐 www.hotelprincipereal.com. MAP P.62–63, POCKET MAP H5 This small four-star sits on a quiet street just below the Bairro Alto. Eighteen rooms, each with modern decor and some with balconies and superb city views. Best of all is the top-floor suite with stunning vistas (€250). **From €145**

THE INDEPENDENTE HOSTEL AND SUITES > Rua de São Pedro de Alcântara 81 🚊 213 461 381, 🌐 www .theindependente.pt. MAP P63, POCKET MAP B10. Highly recommended, this is part hostel and part boutique hotel. The fantastic old building has far-reaching views over Lisbon. Lower floors house dorms (sleeping 6–12), each with towering ceilings. Upstairs are quirky double rooms in the roof spaces, the best with balconies offering river views. There's a downstairs bar and patio and the place offers everything from bar crawls and guided walks to cycle hire. Dorms from €12, doubles from €50

PENSÃO GLOBO > Rua do Teixeira 37, Bus 1 🚊 213 462 279, 🌐 www.cb2web .com/pensaoglobo. MAP P.62–63, POCKET MAP B10 Attractive house on a relatively quiet street, bang in the middle of the Bairro Alto. Fifteen varied rooms: all are simple (including a box room for just €20), though avoid those without windows. There's a bar downstairs. No breakfast. **€40**

PENSÃO LONDRES > Rua Dom Pedro V 53, Bus 1 🚊 213 462 203, 🌐 www .pensaolondres.com.pt. MAP P.62–63, POCKET MAP B10 Wonderful old building with high ceilings and 40 pleasant enough rooms sleeping up to four. Some have tiny bathrooms (€70); those without are cheaper (€40), and the best (ask for rooms 402, 409 or 411) have great views over the city. **From €40**

Estrela, Lapa and Santos

AS JANELAS VERDES > Rua das Janelas Verdes 47, Bus 727 or tram 25 🚊 213 968 143, 🌐 www.heritage .pt. MAP P.75, POCKET MAP G8 This discreet, eighteenth-century townhouse, where Eça de Queirós was inspired to write *Os Maios*, is just metres from the Museu de Arte Antiga. Spacious rooms come with marble bathrooms, period furnishings and most with views of the Tejo. Breakfast is served in the delightful walled garden in summer. The top-floor library and terrace command spectacular river views. **€180**

LAPA PALACE > Rua do Pau da Bandeira 4 🚊 213 949 494, 🌐 www .lapapalace.com. MAP P.75, POCKET MAP F7 A stunning nineteenth-century mansion set in its own lush gardens, with dramatic vistas over the Tejo. Rooms are luxurious, and those in the Palace Wing are each decorated in a different style, from Classical to Art Deco. There's also a health club, disabled access and a list of facilities as long as your arm, from babysitting to banqueting. **€200**

YORK HOUSE > Rua das Janelas Verdes 32, Bus 727 or tram 25 ☎ 213 962 435, ⓦ www.yorkhouselisboa.com. MAP P.75, POCKET MAP G7 Located in a sixteenth-century Carmelite convent (and hidden from the main street by high walls), rooms here are chic and minimalist. The best are grouped around a beautiful interior courtyard, where drinks and meals are served in summer, and there's a highly rated restaurant. Advance bookings recommended. €150

Alcântara and Belém

PESTANA PALACE > Rua Jau 54, Tram 18 ☎ 213 615 600, ⓦ www .pestana.com. MAP P.80–81, POCKET MAP C8 Set in an early twentieth-century palace full of priceless works of art, most beds at this five-star hotel are in tasteful modern wings that stretch either side of lush gardens. Most rooms have large terraces and lie a short walk from a sushi bar, a sunken outdoor pool with a fountain to swim out to, and an indoor pool and health club. The price, which can be greatly reduced for summer offers, includes a vast breakfast in the former ballroom. €215

JERONIMOS 8 > Rua das Jeronimos 8, Tram 15 ☎ 213 600 900, ⓦ www .jeronimos8.com. MAP P.88–89, POCKET MAP C4 In a great position for Belém's attractions, this hotel is an attractive stone building with boutiquey touches – crisp white decor, marble bathrooms and a modern bar area, plus a substantial buffet breakfast. €210

Avenida, Parque Eduardo VII and the Gulbenkian

EUROSTAR DAS LETRAS > Rua Castilho 6–12 Ⓜ Avenida ☎ 213 573 094, ⓦ www.eurostarshotels.com. MAP P.96–97, POCKET MAP H5 Modern hotel with its own small gym and bar in a good position between the centre and the Bairro Alto. Rooms come with comfy beds, a choice of pillows and a complicated

array of power showers. The best have balconies with downtown views. €140

FONTANA PARK > Rua Eng. Viera da Silva 2 Ⓜ Saldanha ☎ 210 410 600, ⓦ www.fontanapark.com. MAP P.96–97, POCKET MAP J3 This buzzy designer hotel rises sleekly behind the facade of an old steelworks. Chic rooms – the best with terraces – come with Philippe Starck chromatic baths. The communal areas include a restaurant, bar and a courtyard garden with slate walls of running water. Cocktail and sushi nights with guest DJs complete the picture. €215

INSPIRA SANTA MARTA > Rua de Santa Marta 48 ☎ 210 440 900, ⓦ www.inspirasantamartahotel.com. MAP P97, POCKET MAP J5. The facade of a traditional townhouse hides a modern boutique hotel which boasts impressive green credentials, including low energy lighting and recycled or local products. Feng-shui designed rooms are compact but comfy with glass-wall showers and – unusually for Lisbon – coffee making facilities and free mini bars. There is also a spa, a games room, a stylish restaurant and bar. €125

HERITAGE LIBERDADE > Avenida da Liberdade Ⓜ Restauradores ☎ 213 404 040, ⓦ www.heritage.pt. MAP P.96–97, POCKET MAP J5 In a superb mansion – whose ground floor once sold herbal remedies (the counter still remains) – this hotel superbly blends tradition and contemporary style. Though the dining area/bar is small (and the gym/plunge pool even smaller), the rooms more than compensate with retro fittings and great cityscapes from top-floor rooms. €190

HOTEL AVENIDA PARK > Avda Sidónio Pais 6 Ⓜ Parque ☎ 213 532 181, ⓦ www.avenidapark.com. MAP P.96–97, POCKET MAP H4 Good-sized rooms – beg for one with a view over the park for no extra charge – in a friendly hotel on a quiet street. €100

HOTEL BRITANIA > Rua Rodrigues Sampaio 17 Ⓜ Avenida ☎ 213 155 016, ⓦ www.heritage.pt. MAP P.96–97, POCKET MAP J5 Designed in the 1940s by influential architect Cassiano Branco, this is an Art Deco gem with huge airy rooms, each with traditional cork flooring and marble-clad bathrooms. The hotel interior, with library and bar, has been declared of national architectural importance .A somewhat pricy breakfast is an extra. €175

HOTEL DOM CARLOS PARQUE > Avda Duque de Loulé 121 Ⓜ Marquês de Pombal ☎ 213 512 590, Ⓦ www .domcarloshoteis.com. MAP P.96–97, POCKET MAP H4 Decent three-star just off Praça Marquês de Pombal, with fair-sized rooms over eight floors, each with cable TV. Some overlook the neighbouring police and fire stations, which can add to the noise. There's a downstairs bar with plasma TV and garage parking. €116.

LISBOA PLAZA > Trav. Salitre 7 Ⓜ Avenida ☎ 213 218 218, Ⓦ www .heritage.pt. MAP P.96–97, POCKET MAP J5 A tasteful, understated former Portuguese family home with marble bathrooms, bar and a fashionable rooftop terrace, a short walk from the main Avenida. Friendly staff and good for families. Limited disabled access. €135

RESIDENCIAL ALEGRIA > Praça da Alegria 12 Ⓜ Avenida ☎ 213 220 670, Ⓦ www.alegrianet.com. MAP P.96–97, POCKET MAP J5 Friendly place in a great position, facing the leafy Praça da Alegria ("Happy Square"). Spacious, brightly coloured rooms with TV, though front ones can be noisy. No breakfast. €78

SANA REX > Rua Castilho 169 Ⓜ Marquês de Pombal/Parque ☎ 213 882 161, Ⓦ www.sanahotels.com. MAP P.96–97, POCKET MAP G4 One of the less outrageously priced hotels in this neck of the woods with small but well-equipped rooms, a bar and its own restaurant. The best rooms are at the front, sporting large balconies overlooking Parque Eduardo VII. €100

SHERATON LISBOA > Rua Latino Coelho 1 Ⓜ Picoas ☎ 213 120 000, Ⓦ www.sheratonlisboa.com. MAP P.96–97, POCKET MAP J3 This 1970s high-rise is something of an icon in this part of Lisbon and is now a mecca for those seeking five star spa facilities. The dated exterior hides some very modern attractions including a heated outdoor pool, swanky rooms and a spectacular top -floor bar and restaurant €120

RESIDENCIAL DOM SANCHO I > Avda da Liberdade 202–2° Ⓜ Avenida ☎ 213 513 160, Ⓦ www.hoteldomsancholisbon .com. MAP P.96–97, POCKET MAP J5 One of the few inexpensive options right on the avenue and, what's more, set in a grand old mansion with high ceilings – though, as you'd expect, the front rooms are noisy. The large, air-conditioned rooms come with satellite TV. €75

NH LIBERDADE > Avda da Liberdade 180B Ⓜ Avenida ☎ 213 514 060, Ⓦ www.nh-hotels.com. MAP P.96–97, POCKET MAP J5 Discreetly tucked into the back of the Tivoli forum shopping centre off the main Avenida, this Spanish chain hotel offers ten floors of modern flair. The best rooms have balconies facing the traditional Lisbon houses at the back. Unusually for central Lisbon, there's a rooftop pool. There's also a bar and restaurant. €155

Sintra

CASA DA VALLE > Rua da Paderna 2 ☎ 219 244 699, Ⓦ www.casadavalle .blogspot.com. MAP P.113. Though steeply downhill from the historic centre, this charming guesthouse still commands unbeatable views across the wooded slopes of Sintra. There are various rooms, from top-floor doubles with the best views, to ground-floor rooms with their own terraces. All rooms access a beautiful garden with its own pool. Good for families, with interconnecting rooms. €90

CHALET RELOGIO > Estrada da Pena 22, Sintra-Vila ☎ 219 241 550, Ⓦ www .chaletrelogio.com. MAP P.113 Architect Luigi Mannini, who worked on the Quinta da Regaleira (see p.115), designed this wonderful mansion with a distinctive clock tower. Rooms are simply furnished but enormous, with big windows and high ceilings, and there's a rambling garden too, though it's a long walk to town and you'll need a car. €65

HOTEL ARRIBAS > Av. A Coelho 28, Praia Grande ☎ 219 289 050, Ⓦ www .hotelarribas.pt. MAP P.113 This modern three-star is plonked ungraciously above the beach. Rooms are giant and come with minibars and satellite TV – those with a sea view are hard to fault. There are also seawater swimming pools, a restaurant and café terrace. Also has family rooms sleeping up to four. Disabled access. €120

HOTEL NOVA SINTRA > Largo Afonso d'Albuquerque 25, Estefânia ☎ 219 230 220, Ⓦ www.novasintra.com. MAP P.113 Very smart *pensão* in a big mansion, whose elevated terrace-café overlooks a busy street. The modern rooms all have cable TV and shiny marble floors, and there's a decent restaurant. €80

HOTEL SINTRA JARDIM > Trav. dos Alvares, São Pedro ☎ & Ⓕ 219 230 738, Ⓦ www.residencialsintra.blogspot.com. MAP P.113 The best mid-range option in the area, this rambling old *pensão* has soaring ceilings, wooden floors and oodles of character. There's a substantial garden with a swimming pool and the giant rooms can easily accommodate extra beds – so it's great for families. Book ahead in summer; in winter there's a log fire in the communal lounge. €80

SÃO SATURNIA > Azóia ☎ 219 289 686, Ⓦ www.saosat.com. MAP P.113 Reached down a steep track – look for the sign left just past the turning to Cabo da Roca, before Azóia – this former convent dates back to the twelfth century and sits in a valley where time seems to stand still. The six rooms, three suites and self-catering apartment are traditionally furnished, while the rambling communal areas are all weathered beams, bare bricks and low ceilings. There's a small outdoor pool, barbecue area, geese, cats, and terraces with stunning views – truly magical. €180

Lisbon coast

HOTEL BAÍA > Avenida Marginal, Cascais ☎ 214 831 033, Ⓦ www .hotelbaia.com. MAP P.124 Large

seafront hotel boasting 113 rooms with a/c and satellite TV; front ones have balconies overlooking the beach. There's a great rooftop terrace complete with a covered pool, and a good restaurant. Parking charged extra. €130/145 with sea view

FAROL DESIGN HOTEL > Avda Rei Humberto II de Italia 7, Cascais ☎ 214 823 490, Ⓦ www.farol.com.pt. MAP P.124 Right on the seafront, this is one of the area's most fashionable hideaways, neatly combining traditional and contemporary architecture. A new designer wing has been welded onto a sixteenth-century villa, and the decor combines wood and marble with modern steel and glass. The best rooms have sea views and terraces. There's also a restaurant, fairy-lit outside bar and seapool facing a fine rocky foreshore. €260, or 315 with sea views

PERGOLA HOUSE > Avda Valbom 13, Cascais ☎ 214 840 040, Ⓦ www .pergolahouse.com. MAP P.124 Sumptuous century-old mansion bang in the centre of town with its own garden, stucco ceilings and wonderfully ornate tiled dining room. Each room has its own distinct character, some with their own balconies. €130

REAL CAPARICA HOTEL > Rua Mestre Manuel 18, Caparica ☎ 212 918 870, Ⓦ www.realcaparicahotel.com. Friendly and reasonable central hotel, a few minutes' walk from the beach, just off Rua dos Pescadores. Small but pleasant rooms come with TV and bath and some have balconies and sea views. €70

SOLAR DOM CARLOS > Rua Latino Coelho 8, Cascais ☎ 214 828 115, Ⓦ www.solardomcarlos.net. MAP P.124 The best-value place in town, set in a sixteenth-century mansion on a quiet backstreet in the pretty western side of Cascais. Dom Carlos once stayed here, hence the royal chapel, which still survives. The tiled interior stays cool in summer, there's a garden and car parking, and the attractive rooms come with satellite TV and fridge. €70

VILA BICUDA > Rua dos Faisões, Cascais ☎ 214 860 200, Ⓦ www .vilabicuda.com. MAP P.124 A very well run, upmarket villa complex set in its own grounds with two large swimming pools. Excellent for families, the modern villas are well equipped and the complex has its own great café, shop and (pricey) Italian restaurant. But you'll need a car – it's around 3km from central Cascais towards Guincho. Studios from €130

Hostels

Lisbon has some of Europe's best independent hostels. A youth hostel card is required for the official Portuguese hostels (*pousadas de juventude*), but you can buy one on your first night's stay. Unless stated, prices do not include breakfast.

CASCAIS BEACH HOSTEL > Rua da Vista Alegre 10, Cascais ☎ 309 906 421, Ⓦ www.cascaisbeachhostel.com. MAP P.124 In a quiet part of town, ten minutes from the centre, this independent hostel has a small pool and garden as well as a communal lounge, kitchen and wi-fi access. Rooms are a good size with or without bath (€20 extra) – the best have small balconies. No breakfast. **Dorm beds €20, doubles from €50**

LISBON LOUNGE HOSTEL > Rua de São Nicolau 13, 4° ⓂRossio ☎213 462 061, Ⓦwww.lisbonloungehostel .com. MAP P.29, POCKET MAP E12 Understandably popular independent hostel in a great old Baixa townhouse full of stripped floorboards, comfy sofas and books. Free wi-fi and breakfast, occasional film screenings and dinner on request. **Dorm beds €25, twins from €35**

OASIS HOSTEL > Rua Santa Catarina 24 Ⓜ Baixa-Chiado/Tram #28 ☎ 213 478 044, Ⓦ www.oasislisboa.com. MAP P.53, POCKET MAP A12 In a lovely old townhouse with its own patio garden – complete with palm tree – this welcoming independent hostel is a stone's throw from the fashionable Miradouro Santa Catarina. **Dorm beds €26, doubles from €66**

POUSADA DE JUVENTUDE DE CATALAZETE > Estrada Marginal, Oeiras ☎ 214 430 638,Ⓦwww .pousadasjuventude.pt. This hostel is set in an eighteenth-century sea-fort overlooking the sea pools in Oeiras, a beach suburb on the train line to Cascais. Reception is open 8am to midnight. Parking available. **Dorms beds €14, twin rooms from €32**

POUSADA DE JUVENTUDE LISBOA PARQUE DAS NAÇÕES > Rua de Moscavide 47–101, Parque das Nações, Ⓜ Oriente ☎ 218 920 890, Ⓦ www .pousadasjuventude.pt. MAP P.107, POCKET MAP A16. About five minutes' walk northeast of the Torre Vasco da Gama, towards the bridge, this smart, modern youth hostel has a pool table and disabled access. **Dorm beds €17, doubles from €45**

POUSADA DE JUVENTUDE DE LISBOA > Rua Andrade Corvo 46 Ⓜ Picoas ☎ 213 532 696, Ⓦ www .pousadasjuventude.pt. MAP P.96–97, POCKET MAP H3 The main city hostel, set in a rambling old building, with a small bar (open 6pm to midnight), canteen, TV room and disabled access. There are 30 dorms sleeping four to six as well as en-suite rooms. Price includes breakfast. **Dorm beds €17, doubles from €45**

TRAVELLERS HOUSE > Rua Augusta 89, 1° Ⓜ Baixa-Chiado ☎ 210 115 922, Ⓦ www.travellershouse.com. MAP P.29, POCKET MAP D12 Right on Lisbon's main pedestrianized street, this award-winning independent hostel has a wonderful high-ceilinged lounge, bean bags and a DVD room. **Dorm beds €28, doubles and studios from €70**

Arrival

Lisbon airport is right on the edge of the city and is well served by buses and taxis. The city's train stations are all centrally located and connected to the metro; the main bus station is also close to metro and train stops.

By air

The aeroporto da Portela (☎ 218 413 700, ⓦ www.aeroportodelisboa.com .pt) is a twenty-minute drive north of the city centre and has a tourist office (daily 7am–midnight, ☎ 218 450 660), a 24hr exchange bureau and left-luggage facilities.

The easiest way in to the centre is by taxi; a journey to Rossio should cost around €15. The airport is also on the red Oriente line of the **metro** (see opposite), although you'll neeed to change at Alameda for the centre. Alternatively, catch #91 **Aerobus** (☎ 966 298 558; daily every 20–30min; from 7am–11pm, €3.55, ticket valid for travel on all city buses for that day) from outside the terminal, which runs to Praça dos Restauradores, Rossio, Praça do Comércio and Cais do Sodré train station. **Local bus** #44 also runs to Praça dos Restauradores and Cais do Sodré station (every 10–15min, €1.75), but is less convenient if you have a lot of luggage.

By train

Long-distance **trains** are run by CP (*Comboios de Portugal*; ☎ 808 208 208, ⓦ www.cp.pt). You'll arrive at Santa Apolónia station, from where you can access the Gaivota metro line or take a bus west to Praça do Comércio. Most trains also call at Oriente station (on the Oriente line) at Parque das Nações This station is more convenient for the airport or northern Lisbon.

By bus

The national **bus** carrier is Rede Expressos (☎ 707 223 344, ⓦ www .rede-expressos.pt). Most services terminate at Sete Rios, next to the Jardim Zoológico metro stop (for the centre) and Sete Rios train line (for Sintra and the northern suburbs). Many bus services also stop at the Oriente station at Parque das Nações on the Oriente metro line.

By car

Apart from weekends, when the city is quiet, **driving** round Lisbon is best avoided, though it is useful to hire a car to see the outlying sights. Parking is difficult in central Lisbon. Pay-and-display spots get snapped up quickly and the unemployed get by on tips for guiding drivers into empty spots. It may be easier heading for an official car park, for which you pay around €2 an hour or €12. Do not leave valuables inside your car.

Getting around

Central Lisbon is compact enough to explore on **foot**, but don't be fooled by the apparent closeness of sights as they appear on maps. There are some very steep hills to negotiate, although the city's quirky elevadores (funicular railways) will save you the steepest climbs. Tram, bus and *elevador* stops are indicated by a sign marked "paragem", which carries route details.

Metro stations (Ⓜ) are located close to most of the main sights. Suburban trains run from Rossio and Sete Rios stations to Sintra and from Cais do Sodré station to Belém, Estoril and Cascais, while ferries (☎ 218 820 348, ⓦ www.transtejo .pt) link Lisbon's Cais do Sodré to Cacilhas, for the resort of Caparica.

The metro

Lisbon's efficient **metro** (*Metro-politano*; daily 6.30am–1am; ☎213 558 457, ⓦwww.metrolisboa.pt) is the quickest way of reaching the city's main sights, with trains every few minutes. Tickets cost €1.25 per journey, or €1.15 with a Viva Viagem card (see below) – sold at all stations (see the inside cover and pull-out map for the network diagram).

Buses and trams

City trams and buses (daily 6.30am–midnight) are operated by Carris (☎213 613 000, ⓦwww.carris.pt). **Buses** (*autocarros*) run just about everywhere in the Lisbon area – the most useful ones are outlined in the box below.

Trams (*eléctricos*) run on five routes, which are marked on the chapter maps. Ascending some of the steepest urban gradients in the world, most are worth taking for the ride alone, especially the cross-city tram #28 (see p.45). Another picturesque route is #12, which circles the castle area via Largo Martim Moniz. Other useful routes are "supertram" #15

Useful bus routes

#201 Night bus from Cais do Sodré to the docks via Santos; until 5am.

#28 Belém to Parque das Nações via Santa Apolónia station.

#737 Praça da Figueira to Castelo de São Jorge via the Sé and Alfama.

#44 Outside the airport to Cais do Sodré via Marquês de Pombal, Avda da Liberdade and the Baixa.

#727 Marquês de Pombal to Belém via Santos and Alcântara.

#773 Rato to Alcântara via Prícipe Real, Estrela and Lapa.

from Praça da Figueira to Belém (signed Algés), and #18, which runs from Rua da Alfândega via Praça do Comércio to the Palácio da Ajuda. The remaining route, #25, runs from Rua da Alfândega to Campo Ourique via Cais do Sodré, Lapa and Estrela (see p.39).

Elevadores

There are also four **elevadores**. These consist of two funicular railways offering quick access to the heights of the Bairro Alto (see p.54 & p.60) and to the eastern side of Avenida da Liberdade (p.33); and one giant lift, the Elevador de Santa Justa (see p.32) which goes up to the foot of the Bairro Alto near Chiado.

Tickets and passes

On board **tickets** cost €1.75 (buses), €2.85 (trams) and €3.50 for *elevadores* (valid for two trips). You need to get a separate card for train lines to Sintra or Cascais. Note that the modern tram #15 has an automatic ticket machine on board and does not issue change.

It's possible just to buy a ticket each time you ride, but **passes**, available from any main metro station, can save you money. First, buy a rechargeable *Viva Viagem* card (€0.50), which you can load up with up to €2–10, after which €1.15 is deducted for each bus or metro journey.

You can also buy a one-day *Bilhete 1dia* pass (€5), which allows unlimited travel on buses, trams, the metro and *elevadores* until midnight of the same day.

If you're planning some intensive sightseeing, the *Cartão Lisboa* (€17.50 for one day, €30 for two days, or €36 for three) is a good buy. The card entitles you to unlimited rides on buses, trams, *elevadores* and the metro as well as entry to or discounts on around 25 museums. It's available from all the main tourist offices.

Sightseeing tours

Open-top bus tour The two-hour "Circuito Tejo" (May–Oct every 30 min from 9.15am–6.45pm; Nov–April every 45min from 9.45am–5.45pm; €15) takes passengers around Lisbon's principal sights; a day-ticket allows you to get on and off whenever you want. The "Olisipo" tour (May–Oct every 45min from 10am–7pm; Nov–March every 45min from 10am–5pm; €15) takes in the Parque das Nações (see p.106). Both tours depart from Praça do Comércio. (Information ☎ 213 582 334, ⓦ www.yellowbustours.com)

Tourist tram tour The "Elétrico das Colinas" (Hills Tour) takes passengers on an eighty-minute ride in an early twentieth-century tram (July–Sept every 20min from 10am–7pm; Oct–June every 30min from 9.45am–6.15pm; €18), departing from Praça do Comércio and touring around Alfama, Chiado and São Bento. (Information on ☎ 213 613 010, ⓦ www.yellowbustours.com)

River cruises Two-and-a-half-hour cruises along the Tejo depart from Praça do Comércio's Estação Fluvial (April–Nov daily at 3pm), stopping at Parque das Nações (when tides permit) and Belém. Tickets (€20, includes drink) valid for returns on the later boats. (Information ☎ 808 203 050, ⓦ www.transtejo.pt)

Sidecar tours Get the lowdown on Lisbon in a motorbike sidecar tour; half-day tours from €60 or €85 for two (☎ 963 965 105, ⓦ www.sidecartouring .co.pt).

Walks Recommended themed two-hour guided walks are offered by Lisbon Walker (☎ 218 861 840, ⓦ www.lisbonwalker.com; €15), departing daily from Praça do Comércio at 10am or 2.30pm, giving expert insight into the quirkier aspects of the city's sites including secret histories and spies.

Taxis

Lisbon's cream **taxis** have a minimum charge of €2.50; an average ride across town is €8–13. Fares are twenty percent higher from 10pm to 6am, at weekends and on public holidays. Bags in the boot incur a €1.60 fee. Meters should be switched on, and tips are not expected. Outside the rush hour taxis can be flagged down quite easily, or head for one of the ranks such as those outside the main train stations. At night, it's best to phone a taxi (attracts an extra charge of €0.80): try Rádio Taxis (☎ 218 119 000), Autocoope (☎ 217 996 460) or Teletáxi (☎ 218 111 100).

Car rental

For more information on driving in Lisbon see p.140. Rental agents include: Auto Jardim, ☎ 213 549 182, airport ☎ 218 462 916, ⓦ www .auto-jardim.com; Avis, ☎ 213 514 560, airport, ☎ 218 435 550, ⓦ www .avis.com; Budget, ☎ 213 860 516, airport ☎ 218 478 803, ⓦ www .budget.com.pt; Europcar, ☎ 213 535 115, airport ☎ 218 401 176, ⓦ www .europcar.com; Hertz, ☎ 219 426 300, ⓦ www.hertz.com.

Directory A–Z

Addresses

Addresses are written in the form "Rua do Crucifixo 50–4°", meaning the fourth storey of no. 50, Rua do Crucifixo. The addition of e, d or r/c at the end means the entrance is on the left (*esquerda*), right (*direita*) or on the ground floor (*rés-do-chão*).

Cinemas

Mainstream **films** are shown at various multiplexes around the city, usually with Portuguese subtitles. Listings can be found on ⓦwww.agendalx.pt/cinema. The Instituto da Cinemateca Portuguesa, Rua Barata Salgueiro ⓜ Avenida (☎ 213 596 266 ⓦwww.cinemateca.pt), the national film theatre, has twice-daily shows and contains its own cinema museum.

Crime

Violent crime is very rare but pickpocketing is common, especially on public transport.

Electricity

Portugal uses two-pin plugs (230/400v). UK appliances will work with a continental adaptor.

Embassies and consulates

Australia, Avda da Liberdade 200–2° ⓜ Avenida; ☎ 213 101 500; Canada, Avda da Liberdade 198–200 ⓜ Avenida; ☎ 213 164 600; Ireland, Rua da Imprensa à Estrela 1–4°, tram #28 to Estrela; ☎ 213 929 440; South Africa, Avda Luís Bivar 10 ⓜ Picoas; ☎ 213 192 200; UK, Rua de São Bernardo 33 ⓜ Rato; ☎ 213 924 000, ⓦwww.uk-embassy.pt; USA, Avda das Forças Armadas, ⓜ Jardim Zoológico; ☎ 217 273 300.

Events listings

The best listings magazine is the free monthly *Agenda Cultural* (ⓦwww.agendalx.pt) produced by the town hall (in Portuguese). *Follow me Lisboa* is an English-language version produced by the local tourist office. Both are available from the tourist offices and larger hotels.

Gay and lesbian travellers

The Centro Comunitário Gay e Lésbico de Lisboa at Rua de São Lázaro 88 (☎ 218 873 918; Wed–Sat 6–11pm, ⓜ Martim Moniz) is the main gay and lesbian community centre, run by ILGA whose website (ⓦwww.ilga-portugal.pt) is in English and Portuguese.

Health

Pharmacies, the first point of call if you are ill, are open Mon–Fri 9am–1pm & 3–7pm, Sat 9am–1pm. Details of **24hr pharmacies** are posted on every pharmacy door, or call ☎ 118. The privately run British Hospital, Rua Tomás da Fonseca (☎ 217 213 400, ⓦwww.gpsaude.pt), has doctors on call 8.30am–9pm. There are various other public hospitals around the city; EU citizens will need form E112.

Internet

Hotels and **internet cafés** charge around €2–4 per hour for access. Useful central options include: Ponto Net, Lisbon Welcome Centre, Praça do Comércio, Baixa (daily 9am–8pm; ☎ 210 312 810) and Web Café, Rua do Diário de Notícias 126, Bairro Alto (daily 4pm–2am; ☎ 213 421 181).

Left luggage

There are 24hr lockers at the airport, main train and bus station, charging around €8 per day.

Lost property

Report any loss to the **tourist police** station in the Foz Cultura building in Palácio Foz, Praça dos Restauradores (daily 24hr ☎ 213 421 634). For items left on public transport, contact Carris ☎ 218 535 403.

Money

Portugal uses the **euro** (€). Banks open Monday to Friday 8.30am–3pm. Most central branches have automatic exchange machines for various currencies. You can withdraw up to €200 per day from ATMs ("Multibanco") – check fees with your home bank.

Opening hours

Most **shops** open Monday to Saturday 9.30am–7pm; smaller shops close for lunch (around 1–2pm) and on Saturday afternoons; shopping centres are open daily until 10pm or later. Most **museums** and **monuments** open Tuesday to Sunday from around 10am–6pm; details are given in the guide.

Phones

Most European-subscribed **mobile phones** will work in Lisbon, though you are likely to be charged extra for incoming and outgoing calls. The cheap rate for national and international calls is 9pm–9am Monday to Friday, and all day weekends and public holidays.

Post

Post offices (*correios*) are usually open Monday to Friday 9am–6.30pm. The main Lisbon office at Praça dos Restauradores 58 is open until 8pm (☎ 213 238 700). Stamps (*selos*) are sold at post offices and anywhere that has the sign "Correio de Portugal – Selos" displayed.

Smoking

In common with most other EU countries, smoking is prohibited in most restaurants and cafés.

Sports

Lisbon boasts two of Europe's top **football** teams, Benfica (Ⓦ www .slbenfica.pt) and Sporting (Ⓦ www .sporting.pt). Fixtures and news on Ⓦ www.uefa.com. The area also contains some of Europe's best **golf courses**, especially around Cascais and Estoril (info at Ⓦ www.portugal golfe.com). The Atlantic beaches at Caparica and Guincho are ideal for **surfing** and windsurfing, and international competitions are frequently held there (details on Ⓦ www.surfingportugal.com). **Horse-riding** is superb in the Sintra hills, and skilled horsemanship can also be seen at Portuguese **bullfights** (see Praça de Touros, p.101). The Estoril Open in April draws **tennis** fans to the city (Ⓦ www.estorilopen.net), and thousands of runners hit the streets for the **Lisbon Marathon** (Ⓦ www .maratonclubedeportugal.com), held in September.

Telephone information

A free telephone information line gives basic tourist information in English (Mon–Sat 9am–midnight, Sun 9am–8pm, ☎ 800 781 212).

Tickets

You can **buy tickets** for Lisbon's theatres and many concerts from the ticket desk in FNAC in the Armazéns do Chiado shopping centre (see p.56), Valentim de Carvalho on Rua do Carmo 28, as well as from the main venues themselves. Online tickets can be purchased from Ⓦ www .ticketline.pt or blueticket.pt.

Time

Portuguese **time** is the same as Greenwich Mean Time (GMT). Clocks go forward an hour in late March and back to GMT in late October.

Tipping

Service charges are included in hotel and restaurant bills. A ten-percent tip is usual for restaurant bills, and hotel porters and toilet attendants expect at least €0.50.

Toilets

There are very few **public toilets** in the streets, although they can be found in nearly all main tourist sights (signed variously as *casa de banho*, *retrete*, *banheiro*, *lavabos* or "WC"), or sneak into a café or restaurant if need be. Gents are usually marked "H" (*homens*) or "C" (*cabaleiros*), and ladies "M" (*mulheres*) or "S" (*senhoras*).

Tourist information

Lisbon's main **tourist office** is the Lisbon Welcome Centre at Praça do Comércio (see map on p.28; daily 9am–8pm; ☎ 210 312 810, ⓦ www.visitlisboa.com), which can supply accommodation lists, bus timetables and maps.

Tourist offices at the airport (see p.140) and at Santa Apolónia station (Tues–Sat 7.30am–1pm, ☎ 218 821 606) can help you find accommodation, as can a few smaller "Ask Me" kiosks dotted around town, like the ones on Rua Augusta and opposite Belém's Mosteiro dos Jerónimos (both daily 10am–1pm & 2–6pm). There is also the Y Lisboa tourist office at Rua Jardim do Regedor 50 (daily 10am–8pm, ☎ 213 472 134), with information geared up to young and student travellers.

There are also tourist offices in all the main **day-trip destinations**: Sintra Turismo (see map, p.113; daily: June–Sept 9am–8pm, Oct–May 9.30am–1.30pm & 2.30–6pm; ☎ 219 231 157, ⓦ www.cm-sintra.pt); Estoril Turismo (opposite the train station; daily: June–Sept 9am–8pm, Oct–May 10am–1pm & 2–6pm; ☎ 214 663 813, ⓦ www.visitestoril.com); Cascais Turismo (see map, p.124; June–Sept Mon–Sat 9am–7pm, Sun 10am–6pm Oct–May 10am–1pm & 2–6pm; ☎ 214 868 204); and Caparica Turismo (Frente Urbana de Praias; Mon–Fri 9.30am–1pm & 2–5.30pm, Sat 9.30am–1pm; ☎ 212 900 071).

Travel agents

The well-informed Top Atlantico, Rua do Ouro 109 (☎ 213 403 220, ⓦ www.topatlantico.pt), Baixa, also acts as an American Express agent.

Travellers with disabilities

Lisbon airport offers a service for **wheelchair-users** if advance notice is given (☎ 213 632 044), while the Orange Badge symbol is recognized for disabled car parking. The main public transport company, Carris, offers an inexpensive dial-a-ride minibus service, *O Serviço Especial de Transporte de Deficientes* (€1.75 per trip; Mon–Fri 6.30am–10pm, Sat & Sun 8am–10pm; ☎ 213 613 141, ⓦ www.carris.pt), though two days' advance notice and a medical certificate are required.

Water

Lisbon's **water** is technically safe to drink, though you may prefer bottled water. Inexpensive bottled water is sold in any supermarket, though tourist shops and restaurants charge considerably more.

Festivals and events

CARNIVAL

February–March

Brazilian-style parades and costumes, mainly at Parque das Nações.

PEIXE EM LISBOA

March–April Ⓦ www.peixemlisboa.com

Lisbon's annual fish festival takes place at the Pátio da Galé in Praça do Comércio and includes masterclasses by top chefs.

ROCK IN RIO LISBOA

May (even yearly) Ⓦ www.rockinrio-lisboa .sapo.pt

Five-day mega rock festival in Parque Bela Vista, in the north of the city.

SANTO ANTONIO

June

Lisbon's main festival is for its adopted saint, Santo António. On June 12 there's a parade down Avenida da Liberdade followed by a giant street party in the Alfama.

GAY PRIDE

June Ⓦ www.arraialpride.ilga-portugal.pt

Lisbon's increasingly popular gay pride event (Arraial Pride) changes venues but has recently been held at Praça do Comércio.

SINTRA MUSIC FESTIVAL

June–July Ⓦ www.estorilportugal.com/events

Performances by international orchestras and dance groups in and around Sintra, Estoril and Cascais.

SUPERBOCK SUPERROCK

July Ⓦ www.superbock.pt

One of the country's largest rock festivals, with local and international bands in various venues, sometimes on the Lisbon coast.

JAZZ EM AUGUSTO

August Ⓦ www.musica.gulbenkian.pt

Big annual (Jazz in August) festival at the Gulbenkian's open-air amphitheatre.

FESTIVAL DOS OCEANOS

August Ⓦ www.festivaldosoceanos.com

A series of concerts and ocean-themed environmental events takes place at various riverside venues throughout August.

SÃO MARTINHO

November 11

St Martin's Day is celebrated with the first tasting of the year's wine accompanied with hot chestnuts.

CHRISTMAS (NATAL)

The main Christmas celebration is midnight Mass on December 24, which is followed by a meal of *bacalhau*.

NEW YEAR'S EVE (ANO NOVO)

The best place for New Year's Eve is Praça do Comércio, where fireworks light up the riverfront.

Public Holidays

In addition to Christmas (Dec 24–25) and New Year's Day public holidays include Shrove Tuesday (Feb/March); Good Friday (March/April); April 25 (Liberty Day); May 1 (Labour Day); June 10 (Portugal/Camões Day); June 12 (Santo António); Feast of the Assumption (Aug 15); Immaculate Conception (Dec 8). Four public holidays, including Independence Day (Dec 1), were scrapped in 2012 in order to promote competitiveness.

Chronology

60 BC > Julius Caesar establishes Olisipo as the capital of the Roman Empire's western colony.

711 > Moors from North Africa conquer Iberia, building a fortress by the *alhama* (hot springs), now known as Alfama.

1147 > Afonso Henriques, the first king of the newly established Portuguese state, retakes Lisbon from the Moors and builds a cathedral on the site of the former mosque.

1495–1521 > The reign of Dom Manuel I coincides with the golden age of Portuguese exploration. So-called "Manueline" architecture celebrates the opening of sea routes. The 1494 Treaty of Tordesillas gives Spain and Portugal trading rights to much of the globe.

1498 > Vasco da Gama returns to Belém with spices from India, which helps fund the building of the monastery of Jeronimos.

1581 > Victorious after the battle of Alcántara, Philip II of Spain becomes Filipe I of Portugal, and Portugal loses its independence.

1640 > Portuguese conspirators storm the palace in Lisbon and install the Duke of Bragança as João IV, ending Spanish rule.

1706–50 > Under João V, gold and diamonds from Brazil kick-start a second golden age; lavish building programmes include the Aqueduto das Águas Livres.

1755 > The Great Earthquake flattens much of Lisbon. The Baixa is rebuilt in "Pombaline" style, named after the Marquês de Pombal.

1800s > Maria II (1843–53) rules with German consort, Fernando II, and establishes the palaces at Ajuda and Pena in Sintra. Fado becomes popular in the Alfama. Avenida da Liberdade is laid out.

1900–10 > Carlos I is assassinated in Lisbon in 1908, while two years later, the exile of Manuel II marks the end of the monarchy and birth of the Republic.

1932–68 > Salazar's dictatorship sees development stagnate. Despite massive rural poverty, elaborate "New State" architecture includes the Ponte 25 de Abril, originally named Ponte de Salazar.

1974 > April 25 marks a largely peaceful Revolution. Former Portuguese colonies are granted independence, leading to large-scale immigration.

1986 > Entry to the European Community enables a rapid redevelopment of Lisbon.

1990s > Lisbon's role as Capital of Culture (1994) and host of Expo 98 helps fund a metro extension, the Ponte Vasco da Gama and the Parque das Nações.

2000–05 > In 2004 Lisbon hosts the European Football Championships. Fado star Mariza brings the music to an international audience.

2005–2015 > EU leaders sign the Lisbon Treaty on Dec 13, 2007, agreeing a draft constitution. Demonstrators take to Lisbon's streets in March 2012, protesting against austerity measures.

Portuguese

English is widely spoken in most of Lisbon's hotels and tourist restaurants, but you will find a few words of Portuguese extremely useful. Written Portuguese is similar to Spanish, though pronunciation is very different. Vowels are often nasal or ignored altogether. The consonants are, at least, consistent:

CONSONANTS

c is soft before e and i, hard otherwise unless it has a cedilla – *açucar* (sugar) is pronounced "assookar".

ch is somewhat softer than in English; *chá* (tea) sounds like Shah.

j is like the "s" in pleasure, as is g except when it comes before a "hard" vowel (a, o and u).

lh sounds like "lyuh".

q is always pronounced as a "k".

s before a consonant or at the end of a word becomes "sh", otherwise it's as in English – Cascais is pronounced "Kashkaish".

x is also pronounced "sh" – Baixa is pronounced "Baisha".

VOWELS

e/é: e at the end of a word is silent unless it has an accent, so that *carne* (meat) is pronounced "karn", while *café* is pronounced "caf-ay".

ã or õ: the tilde renders the pronunciation much like the French -an and -on endings, only more nasal.

ão: this sounds something like a strangled "Ow!" cut off in midstream (as in pão, bread – *são*, saint – *limão*, lemon).

ei: this sounds like "ay" (as in *feito* – finished)

ou: this sounds like "oh" (as in *roupa* – clothes)

Words and phrases

BASICS

sim	yes
não	no
olá	hello
bom dia	good morning
boa tarde/noite	good afternoon/night
adeus	goodbye
até logo	see you later
hoje	today
amanhã	tomorrow
por favor/se faz favor	please
tudo bem?	everything all right?
está bem	it's all right/OK
obrigado/a	thank you (male/ female speaker)
onde	where
que	what
quando	when
porquê	why
como	how
quanto	how much
não sei	I don't know
sabe...?	do you know...?
pode...?	could you...?
há...? (silent "h")	is there...? there is
tem...? pron. "taying")	do you have...?
queria...	I'd like...
desculpe	sorry
com licença	excuse me
fala Inglês?	do you speak English?
não compreendo	I don't understand
este/a	this
esse/a	that
agora	now
mais tarde	later
mais	more
menos	less
grande	big
pequeno	little
aberto	open
fechado	closed
senhoras	women
homens	men
lavabo/quarto de banho	toilet/bathroom

GETTING AROUND

esquerda	left
direita	right
sempre em frente	straight ahead
aqui	here
ali	there
perto	near
longe	far
Onde é...	Where is ...
a estação de camionetas?	the bus station?
a paragem de autocarro para...	the bus stop for...
Donde parte o autocarro para...?	Where does the bus to...leave from?
A que horas parte? (chega a...?)	What time does it leave? (arrive at...?)
Pare aqui por favor	Stop here please
bilhete (para)	ticket (to)
ida e volta	round trip

COMMON SIGNS

aberto	open
fechado	closed
entrada	entrance
saída	exit
puxe	pull
empurre	push
elevador	lift
pré-pagamento	pay in advance
perigo/perigoso	danger/ous
proibido estacionar	no parking
obras	(road) works

ACCOMMODATION

Queria um quarto	I'd like a room
É para uma noite (semana)	It's for one night (week)
É para uma pessoa (duas pessoas)	It's for one person/ two people
Quanto custa?	How much is it?
Posso ver?	May I see/ look?
Há um quarto mais barato?	Is there a cheaper room?
com duche	with a shower

SHOPPING

Quanto é?	How much is it?
banco; câmbio	bank; change
correios	post office
(dois) selos	(two) stamps
Como se diz isto em Português?	What's this called in Portuguese?
O que é isso?	What's that?
saldo	sale
esgotado	sold out

DAYS OF THE WEEK

Domingo	Sunday
Segunda-feira	Monday
Terça-feira	Tuesday
Quarta-feira	Wednesday
Quinta-feira	Thursday
Sexta-feira	Friday
Sábado	Saturday

MONTHS

Janeiro	January
Fevereiro	February
Março	March
Abril	April
Maio	May
Junho	June
Julho	July
Agosto	August
Aetembro	September
Outubro	October
Novembro	November
Dezembro	December

USEFUL WORDS

azulejo	glazed, painted tile
cais	quay
capela	chapel
casa	house
centro commercial	shopping centre
estação	station
estrada/rua	street/road
feira	fair or market
igreja	church
jardim	garden
miradouro	viewpoint/belvedere
praça/largo	square

NUMBERS

um/uma	1
dois/duas	2
três	3
quatro	4
cinco	5
seis	6
sete	7
oito	8
nove	9
dez	10
onze	11
doze	12
treze	13
catorze	14
quinze	15
dezasseis	16
dezassete	17
dezoito	18
dezanove	19
vinte	20
vinte e um	21
trinta	30
quarenta	40
cinquenta	50
sessenta	60
setenta	70
oitenta	80
noventa	90
cem	100
cento e um	101
duzentos	200
quinhentos	500
mil	1000

Food and drink terms

BASICS

assado	roasted
colher	spoon
conta	bill
copo	glass
cozido	boiled
ementa	menu
estrelado/frito	fried
faca	knife
garfo	fork
garrafa	bottle
grelhado	grilled
mexido	scrambled

MENU TERMS

pequeno almoço	breakfast
almoço	lunch
jantar	dinner
ementa turística	set menu
prato do dia	dish of the day
especialidades	speciality
lista de vinhos	wine list
entradas	starters
petiscos	snacks
sobremesa	dessert

SOUPS, SALAD AND STAPLES

açucár	sugar
arroz	rice
azeitonas	olives
batatas fritas	chips/french fries
caldo verde	cabbage soup
fruta	fruit
legumes	vegetables
massa	pasta
manteiga	butter
molho (de tomate/ piri-piri)	tomato/chilli sauce
omeleta	omelette
ovos	eggs
pão	bread
pimenta	pepper
piri-piri	chilli sauce
queijo	cheese
sal	salt
salada	salad
sopa de legumes	vegetable soup
sopa de marisco	shellfish soup
sopa de peixe	fish soup

FISH AND SHELLFISH

atum	tuna
camarões	shrimp
carapau	mackerel
cherne	stone bass
dourada	bream
espada	scabbard fish
espadarte	swordfish
gambas	prawns

lagosta	lobster
lulas (grelhadas)	squid (grilled)
mexilhões	mussels
pescada	hake
polvo	octopus
robalo	sea bass
salmão	salmon
salmonete	red mullet
santola	spider crab
sapateira	crab
sardinhas	sardines
tamboril	monkfish
truta	trout
viera	scallop

MEAT

alheira	chicken sausage
borrego	lamb
chanfana	lamb or goat casserole
chouriço	spicy sausage
coelho	rabbit
cordeiro	lamb
dobrada/tripa	tripe
espetada mista	mixed meat kebab
febras	pork steaks
fiambre	ham
fígado	liver
frango no churrasco	barbecued chicken
leitão	roast suckling pig
pato	duck
perdiz	partridge
perú	turkey
picanha	strips of beef in garlic sauce
presunto	smoked ham
rim	kidney
rodizio	barbecued meats
rojões	cubed pork cooked in blood with potatoes
vitela	veal

PORTUGUESE SPECIALITIES

açorda	bread-based stew (often seafood)
arroz de marisco	seafood rice
bife à portuguesa	thin beef steak with a fried egg on top
caldeirada	fish stew
bacalhau à brás	salted cod with egg and potatoes
bacalhau na brasa	dried cod roasted with potatoes
bacalhau a Gomes Sá	dried cod baked with potatoes, egg and olives
cataplana	fish, shellfish or meat stewed in a circular metal dish
cozido à portuguesa	boiled casserole of meat and beans, served with rice and vegetables
feijoada	bean stew with meat and vegetables
migas	meat or fish in a bready garlic sauce
porco à alentejana	pork cooked with clams

SNACKS AND DESSERTS

arroz doce	rice pudding
bifana	steak sandwich
bolo	cake
gelado	ice cream
pastel de nata	custard tart
pastéis de bacalhau	dried cod cakes
prego	steak sandwich
pudim	crème caramel

DRINKS

um copo/uma garrafa de/da...	a glass/bottle of...
vinho branco/tinto	white/red wine
cerveja	beer
água (sem/com gás)	mineral water (without/with gas)
fresca/natural	chilled/room temperature
sumo de laranja/ maçã	orange/apple juice
chá	tea
café	coffee
sem/com leite	without/with milk
sem/com açúcar	without/with sugar

PUBLISHING INFORMATION

This second edition published April 2013 by **Rough Guides Ltd**

80 Strand, London WC2R 0RL

11, Community Centre, Panchsheel Park, New Delhi 110017, India

Distributed by the Penguin Group

Penguin Books Ltd, 80 Strand, London WC2R 0RL

Penguin Group (USA) 375 Hudson Street, NY 10014, USA

Penguin Group (Australia) 250 Camberwell Road, Camberwell, Victoria 3124, Australia

Penguin Group (NZ) 67 Apollo Drive, Mairangi Bay, Auckland 1310, New Zealand

Rough Guides is represented in Canada by Tourmaline Editions Inc. 662 King Street West, Suite 304, Toronto, Ontario M5V 1M7

Typeset in Minion and Din to an original design by Henry Iles and Dan May.

Printed and bound in China

© Matthew Hancock 2013

Maps © Rough Guides

160pp includes index

A catalogue record for this book is available from the British Library

ISBN 978-1-40936-242-5

ROUGH GUIDES CREDITS

Text editor: Andy Turner

Layout: Dan May and Umesh Aggarwal

Cartography: Katie Bennett

Picture editors: Mark Thomas and Rhiannon Furbear

Photographers: Matthew Hancock and Natascha Sturny

Production: Linda Dare

Proofreader: Jan McCann

Cover design: Sarah Ross

MIX
Paper from
responsible sources
FSC™ C018179
www.fsc.org

THE AUTHOR

Matthew Hancock fell in love with Portugal when he was a teacher in Lisbon. He later returned to the country to walk the 775-mile Portuguese-Spanish border. Now a journalist and editor living in Dorset, he is also the author of the Rough Guides to the Algarve and Madeira and co-author of the *Rough Guide to Portugal* and the *Rough Guide to Dorset, Hampshire and the Isle of Wight*.

ACKNOWLEDGEMENTS

Thanks to everyone who helped, especially Vítor Carriço at Visit Lisboa, Paula Quintas at Hotel do Chiado, Gonçalo Dias at LX Boutique, José Salavisa and Nelly Correia at CS Hotels, Sandra Mencucci at Inspira Hotels, Dave Palethorpe at Cinco Lounge, José Avillez, Luke and Paula Tilley Pimenta; Amanda, Alex and Olivia for their usual support, and to everyone at Rough Guides, especially Andy Turner.

HELP US UPDATE

We've gone to a lot of effort to ensure that the first edition of **Pocket Rough Guide Lisbon** is accurate and up-to-date. However, things change – places get "discovered", opening hours are notoriously fickle, restaurants and rooms raise prices or lower standards. If you feel we've got it wrong or left something out, we'd like to know, and if you can remember the address, the price, the hours, the phone number, so much the better.

Please send your comments with the subject line "**Pocket Rough Guide Lisbon Update**" to **@** mail@roughguides.com. We'll credit all contributions and send a copy of the next edition (or any other Rough Guide if you prefer) for the very best emails.

Have your questions answered and tell others about your trip at **@** www.roughguides.com

READERS' LETTERS

Thanks to all the readers who have taken the time to write in with comments and suggestions (and apologies if we have inadvertently omitted or misspelt anyone's name):
Peter Gilbert; John Shayer; Maggie Hills; Clifford Ransom II; Virginia Waite

PHOTO CREDITS

All images © Rough Guides except the following:

Front cover Tram, Alfama district © Romain Cintract/Hemis/Axiom

Back cover Rua Garrett/Largo do Chaido © Renaud Visage/Corbis

p.1 View over the Alfama district © Banana Pancake/Alamy

p.2 Decorative pavement, Rossio Square © Carlos S Pereyra/Superstock

p.4 Rua Augusta © Michele Falzone/Corbis

p.5 Terraco Bar © Michele Falzone/Corbis

p.6 Igreja de Santa Engracia © Yadid Levy/Corbis

p.8 Pasteis de Nata © Michele Falzone/Corbis

p.8 Tram #28 © Mark Thomas

p.9 Torre de Belém © PCI/Alamy

p.9 Bairro Alto nightlife © Andy Christiani/Alamy

p.11 Oceanário © Hans Georg Roth/Corbis

p.11 Palácio da Pena © Marco Simoni/Getty Images

pp.13–14 Padrão dos Descobrimentos map © Mark Thomas

p.15 Mosteiro dos Jerónimos © Gustavo Figueiredo/ Turismo de Lisboa

p.15 Castelo de São Jorge © Gustavo Figueiredo/ Turismo de Lisboa

p.17 The Temptations of St Anthony by Hieronymous Bosch © MNAA

p.17 Casa das Histórias © Luis Ferreira Alves

p.19 Grilled prawns © Sean Russell/ Getty Images

p.20 Lux nightclub © Luisa Ferreira/Lux Club

p.21 Portas Largas bar © LOOK/Alamy

p.24 Mercado da Ribeira © Yadid Levy/Alamy

p.25 Manuel Tavares © Cro Morgan/Alamy

pp.26–27 Mosteiro dos Jerónimos © Marco Simoni/Corbis

p.31 View over the Baxia District © Luis Veiga/ Getty Images

p.32 Elevador de Santa Justa © Mark Thomas

p.33 Elevador do Lavra © Mark Thomas

p.64 Bairro Alto nightlife © Forget Gautier/ Alamy

p.72 Solar do Vinho do Porto, Lisbon © Pedro Moura/Port and Douro Wines Institute

p.73 Traditional fado guitar © Turismo de Lisboa/ Gustavo Figueiredo

p.74 Basílica Estrela © Sylvain Grandadam/ Corbis

p.76 Museu Nacional de Arte Antigua © MMNA

p.81 Museu do Oriente interior © Meseu do Oriente

p.90 Torre de Belém © Mark Thomas

p.91 Padrão dos Descobrimentos © Tobias Titz/fstop/Corbis

p.101 Praça de Touros © Martin Jones/Corbis

p.103 Eleven restaurant © Eleven Restaurant

p.116 Palácio da Pena © Marco Simoni/Corbis

p.123 Estoril beach © Rolf Richardson/Robert Harding World Imagery/Corbis

pp.138–139 Rossio Station © Mark Thomas

Index

Maps are marked in **bold**.

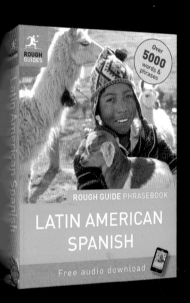